VERY

The Native's Guide to the Best of Los Angeles

David Hoffman

Chronicle Books ~ San Francisco

Printed in the United States of America.

Library of Congress Cataloging in Publication Data
Hoffman, David, 1953–
Very LA: the native's guide to the best of Los Angeles / David Hoffman.
p. cm.
Includes index.
ISBN 0-87701-572-4
1. Los Angeles (Calif.)— Description—Guidebooks.
2. Los Angeles (Calif.)— Popular culture.
F869.L83H64 1989 88-32342
917.94'940453—dc19 CIP

Editing: Marcella Friel
Book and cover design: Triad, San Rafael, California

10 9 8 7 6 5 4 3 2 1

Acknowledgments

Trying to say thanks for help in putting together a book like this could be unending when you realize that the information it contains is a mix of having lived in a place for 14 years and the end result of every blurb ever read, every hot tip passed on, and every secret find shared.

Still, there are those who, in one way or another, made putting together these particular pages a hell of a lot easier. So thanks to:

... KABC and *AM Los Angeles* for letting me turn my vices to profit by paying me (for three years, yet) to shop, eat, travel, hang out, and just do what I normally do; and particularly to Bob Levitan, who launched my regular spot, and to Beth Forcelledo, who later stopped it. God knows if she hadn't fired me, I never would have had time to put all this down on paper.

... Bill LeBlond and Mary Ann Gilderbloom at Chronicle Books, for their support, patience (okay, so the manuscript was a little late . . .) and willingness to let me have (or at least think I was having) the final word.

... Mom and Dad, who in 14 years never once said, "Give it up, move back home, and be a doctor." . . . probably knowing damn well that a book called *Very Richmond* would have been a difficult sell.

☎ All phone numbers listed without an area code are within area code 213.

Chronicle Books
275 Fifth Street
San Francisco, California
94103

Contents

Contents

Introduction

I love LA.

There, I've said it. I couldn't always. For years I bit my tongue, hid the truth, kept my feelings to myself, fearing what my friends and family would think.

It was May 1974 when we first met. From the moment I laid eyes on her, she threw me. Sure, she was beautiful, but she also had no heart. Quite a switch from the others I had known before her. With them, there wasn't any doubting where I stood. But this one was a tease. For an entire summer, she led me on. She was a series of freeways, promising one thing, then going someplace else, careful not to let me get too close. So I left.

The memories didn't. They stayed with me, got better in time. And six months later, when she suggested I come back, I hopped the next plane out. Okay, so I was young.

Some things about her hadn't changed: her smog, her traffic, her tremors. But I put aside my preconceived notions. I agreed not to expect too much of her, when all she asked of me was my own set of wheels and an answering machine.

Her self-esteem was enviable. She did exactly what she wanted, thumbing her nose at everyone else. Yes, she was flaky, wishy-washy, but never without charm. Her spirit was infectious. I grew to laugh with her, not at her, and gradually she let me see a softer side.

First, it was only those things I'd heard tell about, as if she had to prove a point: lavish picnics at the Bowl, a visit to the Getty, the gingerbread houses on Carroll Avenue. But eventually her whole personality emerged. She wasn't just all making movies and Melrose. She was a melting pot of cultural and culinary riches. She was hard bodies with perpetual tans and hard-working immigrants grateful for a second chance. She had style. She could be sassy, silly, serious. She was historically significant yet terminally trendy.

It was a struggle, but it was worth it . A good relationship always is. Oh, I know I'm not the only one. Nor will I ever be. I realized that the day that I moved in. But as long as she continues to make me laugh, to ease the tough times, and love me back, I'll be around.

"They're heeere...."

What to Do With, Where to Take, How to Handle Out-of-Town Guests

1

Best Bets for Tourists, Helpful Hints for Hosts

Experts predict that 50 million tourists will visit the Los Angeles area this year. Sometimes it will feel like they all plan on staying with you.

Best Deal on a Set of Wheels

Bob Leech Auto Rental Chances are your guests are going to decide they want a car. While they won't be able to touch anything at the majors for under $40, Leech rents brand-new and late-model Toyotas (two-door, four-door, and wagons) for just $15.95 a day. Better yet, he charges only $3 for the insurance, he won't gouge them on the gas, and should they want to drive up to San Francisco, he'll let them drop it off without any extra charge. 4490 W. Century Boulevard, LA; (800) 635-1240.

Note: Some smaller rental car chains, like **RPM** (800-367-4776) and **Thrifty** (800-367-2277), frequently offer bargain weekly rates at their airport locations, often as low as $69 a week. The catch is that customers have to pay through the nose for the insurance (easily as much as $13 a day), but if your guests have a credit card (American Express, for example) that offers free collision coverage, it can be quite a deal. And should they just want a car for the weekend (and you don't want to have to schlep them down to the airport to pick it up), **Enterprise** (800-325-8007), with numerous locations throughout the LA area, advertises a three-day special (from anytime on Friday until the same time Monday) for a flat rate of $49.95, with 450 free miles.

Best Places to Sleep Cheap
... when you don't have the room

Hilgard House Hotel Steps away from the UCLA campus, this small, pleasant hotel offers rooms with window seats and Queen Anne furnishings, bathrooms with double sinks and jacuzzi tubs, rates ($75 to $100) that are at least half of those at the Westwood Marquis across the street, and an unbelievable weekend special—Friday and Saturday nights for $119 total—that is applicable even when guests plan on staying longer. There is no restaurant or bar, but a continental breakfast is sent to the room each morning and more traditional room service is possible (and available) courtesy of the 80 or so eateries in nearby Westwood Village. All of the above and free parking, too. 927 Hilgard Avenue, Westwood; 208-3945 or (800) 826-3934.

Beverly House Hotel Travel experts claim that the foremost criterion in choosing a hotel is its location. And locations don't get any better than this. Tucked away on the edge of the Beverly Hills flats, and within easy walking distance of Rodeo Drive, the Beverly House is reminiscent of an old-fashioned European pension. Remodeled in 1984, the rooms ($78 to $98) are tiny and unpretentious, but not without comfort—from the Thomasville furniture and overstuffed quilts to the minirefrigerators and VCRs. Popular with the woman business traveler, and perfect for the in-laws who don't want to impose on the kids. 140 S. Lasky Drive, Beverly Hills; 271-2145.

Marymount College Housing Office It isn't a hotel, but families with kids, groups of students, or couples traveling together should know that during June, July, and August, the Marymount College Housing Office in Palos Verdes can arrange to rent them completely furnished, school-operated, off-campus apartments on a nightly, weekly, or monthly basis. One-, two-, and three-bedroom plans are available, each with a full-sized kitchen. Prices range from $36 to $105, and all guests have access to both swimming pools and tennis courts. 377-5501, x220.

Hollywood on Location While all the other tourists are paying primo prices to stand in line at Universal, yours should be heading here. Every weekday morning at 9:30, Jack Weinberg's company publishes a detailed list of the various (usually 20 to 30) feature films, TV series, movies of the week, and rock videos that will be shooting on location in the LA area that day. For $29, they are given a package that spells out the names and addresses of the different productions, the stars who are involved, the stunts and special effects that have been scheduled — along with an easy-to-follow set of maps and directions so that they can guide their own tour. Not only is it a guaranteed way to get a behind-the-scenes look at how Hollywood works, but tell them to be patient and to stay out of the way, and chances are they'll leave with a much better photo than one of the family standing next to a mechanical shark. 8644 Wilshire Boulevard, Beverly Hills; 659-9165.

> **Best Way to See the Magic of the Movies**

Spago Yes, Spago. And here's how: first, make a reservation, but only for 11:00 P.M. or later. Then show up at 10:30, have a drink at the bar, and check out the crowd. Later, when you sit down to eat, ask the waiter to bring you a dessert platter. You see, Spago makes all their own desserts (and wonderful desserts at that) and at the end

> **Best Restaurant for Star Gazing**
> *... even on a budget*

of each night (the kitchen closes at 11:30), they want to get rid of them. Which is good news for you, because except on a rare evening when too many late dinners are booked, they will happily let you camp out at a table and polish off a generous assortment of pastries, cakes, tarts, tortes, homemade ice cream, and fresh fruit. The bill for a party of four, including coffee, won't be much more than $40. And no telling what famous face will be sitting at the table next to you, eyeing the selection and only too eager to ask you and your guests for a bite. 8795 Sunset Boulevard, W. Hollywood; 652-4025.

Best Place to Buy Souvenirs

The Disney Store A godsend when you don't have time for Disneyland, don't plan to go to Disneyland, or don't want to fork over $21.50 to get in just so *they* can pick up a Mickey Mouse or two. The difference between these three swell shops and the dozens of Disneyland boutiques overpopulating the department stores and malls is that a good 80 percent of the merchandise is "park exclusive"—character-related items (from kitsch to collectible) that before now were solely available in Anaheim or Orlando. And not only are the outlets owned by Disney, but the staff is hired in the same manner as the kids who work at the park (i.e., through the studio), so you can bet there are no surly clerks or ugly attitude problems. While they do stock "ears" (and even an occasional Disneyland pin or pen), for that official Disneyland sweatshirt, you'll still have to hit the real place. Glendale Galleria, Glendale; (818) 247-0222. Other locations: South Coast Plaza, Costa Mesa; Del Amo Fashion Center, Torrance.

Best Place to 'Do' LA

Sunset Boulevard Covering 27 miles—from the barrio to the beach—a ride down this legendary street is a fast-moving collage of what life in Los Angeles is all about. Start north of downtown (yes, Virginia, there *is* a downtown, complete with hotel towers, office complexes, art museums, and theaters) at the point where Olvera Street, Chinatown, and Little Tokyo converge. Head west, bypassing Dodger Stadium and passing through an enclave of poorer Latino neighborhoods.

Enter Silverlake, the inner-city version of Venice, currently undergoing renewed growth and renovation thanks to a healthy influx of artists, two-career couples, and gays. If time allows, circle around the reservoir, where houses built into the sloping landscape are reminiscent of a Mediterranean hill town; have breakfast at **Millie's** (3524 Sunset, 662-5720), just eight stools at a counter (plus a stray table or two), a favorite place for homemade biscuits, spicy eggs, and perfectly greasy cottage fries.

Cross into Hollywood, at first a blend of seediness and sleaze, later a living history: **The Hollywood Palladium** (6215 Sunset), the home of the big bands in the '40s and *The Lawrence Welk Show* in the '60s; **The Aquarius Theater** (6230 Sunset), site of *Queen for a Day;* the **Cinerama Dome** (6360 Sunset), the first theater built to accommodate the extra-wide screens of the Cinerama process; and **Hollywood High** (at Highland Avenue), alma mater of Carol Burnett, Linda Evans, Stephanie Powers, and Ricky Nelson.

Then mousse your hair and cruise the Sunset Strip, where a bastion of one-of-a-kind billboards serves as backdrop to the chorus line of hip hotels (the **Chateau Marmont,** where Garbo stayed and Belushi died), boutiques (along **Sunset Plaza**), restaurants (**Spago, Le Dome,** and **Duke's Coffee Shop,** among them), and clubs (**The Comedy Store**). If you're hungry, grab a bite at **Chin Chin** (8618 Sunset; 652-1818)—the hottest thing to hit the area since "Kookie" Byrnes was lending girls his comb — be sure to take in the great view from the parking lot in back before heading in and chowing down on Szechuan dumplings and Chinese chicken salad.

Next come the palaces of Beverly Hills, which will impress you with their stately portals and manicured lawns, and depress you when you figure that most of the luxury cars outside them are alone probably worth more than your house. Don't miss **The Beverly Hills Hotel** (see "LA Landmarks"), a pink-and-green monument to country-club living, and the mansion at **10100**, with its whimsical statues dotting the front drive.

Wind your way around the park-like north campus of UCLA, past exclusive Bel Air, its wealth hidden by trees and high walls, over the freeway and through Brentwood, envied for space, greenery, and unpretentious affluence. When you reach Pacific Palisades, the clean air, chic bucolic canyons, and grassy Will Rogers State Park (where they hold polo matches on the weekends) will get you primed for the final beauty left to come: the descent down to the ocean in time to watch the sunset. Ah, yes, just another perfect day in LA.

2

LA Laws

*A tourist's guide to going
native in six easy steps*

**Step 1:
Eschew Public
Transportation**

In LA you are what you drive. And clearly, the quintessential LA car is the convertible. While most rental agencies stock the latest models as part of their inventory, **Dreamboats** (8536 Wilshire Boulevard, 659-3277) offers only America's classics. For $49 to $99 a day (with 50 free miles), you can rent the best of the breed, from a pink '59 Caddy to a '63 T-bird or '65 Mustang. So put down the top, crank up the Beach Boys, and ride off into the sunset. Sunset Boulevard, that is.

**Step 2:
Work Out**

We're talking about a city with a gym, health spa, Nautilus club, fitness center, or aerobics studio on every corner (and a private trainer in every home). So, when in Rome. . . . Sure you could pump iron with Schwarzenegger at Gold's, but the quintessential day of exercise (super-hype and all) is still at Jane Fonda's **Workout** (369 S. Robertson Boulevard, Beverly Hills; 652-9464). If you're lucky, you may hit it when the lady herself is teaching (single classes run $8.50), but if not, you could still find yourself "going for the burn" alongside the likes of Streisand or Madonna.

**Step 3:
Do Lunch**

They power breakfast and graze for dinner, but the paramount LA meal is lunch. And while you could choose to make the scene at Citrus or be seen at Le Dome, the quintessential lunch place is **The Ivy** (113 N. Robertson Blvd., W. Hollywood; 274-8303). At first glance, the country-manor look (complete with open hearths, weathered antiques, and hand-painted pottery) and the mostly American menu seem atypical of other slick, sleek in-spots around town. But the array of celebrities and wannabes (and just a lot of pretty people) will satisfy one basic requirement ("I want to see movie stars"), and the sunlit bi-level patio will fulfill the other ("I want to eat outside"). The anadama bread, the Louisiana crabcakes, and the desserts are enough to make anybody happy.

Step 4: Shop

The biggest problem with shopping in LA is that from the Banana Republic to the Sharper Image, many of the stores that were once "so California" have now been branched off, franchised, sold, and cloned. So wave good-bye to Westwood and bypass Beverly Hills (Neiman-Marcus can mail order, thank you). The quintessential place to shop is at **Fred Segal** (8100 Melrose Avenue, LA; 651-4129), the Grandfather of Melrose stores and not just one store, but an unfolding strip of up-to-the-minute shops (Fred Segal Feet), boutiques (Fred Segal Sportswear), departments (Fred Segal Gadget), and stalls (Fred Segal Eats) that occupy the whole block. For the forever trendy, the annual September sale (prices start at 50 percent off) can be worth the plane fare back. Yes, yes . . . there is another Fred Segal store in Santa Monica, and while it's no slouch on the hip scale, its all-enclosed, mini-mall feel does make it second to the original.

You'll find celebrity gossip in every newspaper and on every talk show around town. But face it. Will anyone really be impressed when all you can tell them is about some indie prod who inked a deal for a three-pic pact? So put down the trades, turn off the tube, and pick up a free copy of **The Hollywood Kids** (available all over town; call 659-1477). Cut and pasted, hand-stapled, and looking like a junior high newspaper (down to the Instamatic photos), this self-published, every-other-week underground magazine is littered with blind items and more inside dirt than a Hoover upright. Besides who's seeing who, it's who's suing who, who did what (with what), who's on what, who was where, and why who else wasn't. Even if only ten percent of this stuff is true, with the best skinny on the Hollywood hunk who favors ladies undies, or the famous female singer who simply favors ladies, you'll be the most popular guest at the party.

Step 5: Gossip

Inasmuch as the margarita has become the unofficial drink of LA, you should probably know that you can find the trendiest one at **City** (made with Chinaco tequila, Cointreau, and fresh lime), the cheapest one at **El Coyote** (a buck a pop), and the most classic ones at **El Cholo** (two points for history) and **Lucy's El Adobe** (frothy without the slush, and quietly stiff).

Step 6: Have a Drink and Watch the Sunset

Still, LA is not a city obsessed with meeting for a drink after work, probably because it is a city run by a business where most people are constantly out of work. Rather, the image is of a culture on chaise lounges, sipping cocktails by the pool. And while there's not a pool in sight, the quintessential place to sip away (as the sun slips away) is **Geoffrey's** (27400 Pacific Coast Highway, Malibu; 457-1519). The food is only okay (and definitely overpriced), but the restaurant sits on a cliff overlooking the Pacific, and the large outdoor terrace winding around the edge serves up the most picture-postcard–perfect ocean view in town.

3 A Guide to Unusual Guided Tours

*For the out-of-towner weary of
LA logistics, why not leave
the driving (and the planning)
to someone else?*

Get the Picture

Art Safaris From Venice to downtown, in the last
few years, LA's contemporary art scene has exploded.
Collector/enthusiast Lorel Cornman leads individuals
and groups (via limousine or minivan) through the maze
of galleries, lofts, and studios and plans a range of special
events (ask her about "At Home with Art"). Artists and
gallery directors are often present at stops along the way
to talk with you, discuss their work, tour you through
the backrooms, and answer your questions. Additionally,
Art Safaris offers special Sunday expeditions to major
museums in Los Angeles, Santa Barbara, and La Jolla,
and with enough advance notice, can design your tour
to order (call for prices). Best yet, should you wish to
buy, Cornman is a whiz who will happily advise and
consult. 479-7077.

Get a Foothold

The Conservancy Tours For anyone who believes that
the best way to see a city is on foot, the Los Angeles
Conservancy, dedicated to the preservation of endangered
landmarks and historical buildings, does the unthinkable
and offers six different (and equally delightful) walking
tours of LA. At least three of the series are available on
any given Saturday; the cost is minimal ($5) and advance
reservations are required. You'll explore art deco LA, ven-
ture through the classic old movie houses on Broadway,
or rediscover the magnificent Seventh Street shopping dis-
trict, much of which is currently being renovated and
restored. 623-TOUR, information; 623-CITY, reservations.

**Get It
Wholesale**

Geri Cook's Shopping Tours Originator of LA's *Best
Bargains* newsletter and telephone hotline, Cook mainly
organizes her tours for women's groups, but die-hard
shoppers will be pleased to know that once a month or so,
she plots out day-long expeditions that are open to the
public. For $25, you and a busload of fellow mallbusters
will scour the city—from the westside or the valley to
downtown and Orange County—stopping at six to eight
heretofore unknown stores (outlets, warehouses, businesses) offering the best buys around on name-brand
clothing, jewelry, linens, crystal, china, kitchenware, and

more. A gourmet box lunch is included, served "on board, as you go," so no need to worry about losing valuable time while someone in the group lingers over cigarettes and coffee. 203-9233.

Grave Line Tours Satisfy your morbid curiosity and mourn the death of Hollywood (literally) with a close-up look at the sites and scenes of Tinseltown's most notorious "deaths, sins, and scandals." Greg Smith will squire you around (in a gray Cadillac hearse, no less), as he points out the carport where Sal Mineo was fatally stabbed, lets you ponder the state of romance at Marilyn Monroe's bedroom window, and takes you to the very spot where Cheryl Crane decided Johnny Stompanato had gone far enough. Sure, the two-and-a-half hour tour (tickets run $25 to $30) can attract a Bud Cort or two, but basically, this one's for hipsters. Baby Boomers take note. 392-5501.

Get Real

The California Native Former university professor Lee Klein is the Garry Shandling of the tour-guide world, mixing a great repartee with amusing anecdotes, historical information, and a day-long trip to "the other Los Angeles" (more commonly known as the desert). You'll walk through Devil's Punchbowl, follow the San Andreas fault, climb Vasquez Rocks, see where gold was first discovered in California. Go alone or form your own group; "adventures" are limited to 14 people and tickets average $55. 642-1140.

Get Outta Dodge

LA Nighthawks Sorting out what to do during the day can be bad enough, but having to plan a night on the town is the worst. So don't. Let Charles Andrews and staff do it for you. Be it for two or two hundred, Andrews' Nighthawks will lead you on an insider's tour of LA after dark—starting with dinner, then on to two or three of the city's top comedy, jazz, or dance clubs. The evening— complete with car, driver and guide, plus all dinners, drinks and cover charges—can run anywhere from $550 for two to $800 for seven, depending on how many go and where you want to be seen. For those who don't have the patience to wait in line or who want access to the underground/semiprivate club scene without the intimidation, this is it. 859-1171.

Get a Table

Culinary Adventures See "Unusual Classes, Courses, and Clubs."

Mentioned Elsewhere

4

LA Landmarks

1. Bullock's Wilshire Shop till you drop at this drop-dead gorgeous art deco department store. The merchandise selection plays second fiddle to the zigzag green crown and period detail. With its main entrance at the rear, adjacent to the parking lot instead of the street, this was LA's first suburban shopping experience, clearly designed for the automobile rather than the pedestrian. Explore the interior, then join the ladies who lunch for finger sandwiches, fashion shows, and old-fashioneds at the tea room on the fifth floor. 3050 Wilshire Boulevard, LA; 382-6161.

2. The Beverly Hills Hotel Granted there are other hotels that are prettier, more perfect, or more private (the Bel-Air and the St. James, for example), but this pink-and-green stucco palace reigns supreme as the unofficial (and superficial) symbol of LA's casual chic. Still, you don't have to know someone (or even be staying here) to soak up your share of the hedonistic lifestyle. The counter-only **Fountain Coffee Room** downstairs is one of Beverly Hill's best-kept lunch-place secrets; the near-perfect drug-store-style cheeseburger (washed down with an incomparable orange freeze), though somewhat pricey for coffee-shop fare, will afford you the chance to wander the tropical grounds and take a peek at the legendary pool and Polo Lounge. Before you leave, stop and "say cheeeese" amid the palm, banana, and jacaranda tree-dotted landscape, the perfect setting for a commemorative vacation picture, Robin Leach–style. 9641 Sunset Boulevard, Beverly Hills; 276-2251.

3. David Hockney Swimming Pool Not just another pretty pool, this is one that has definitely made a splash. But what else would you expect when a local resident, known worldwide for his paintings of swimming pools, decides to literally paint one? The results are a fitting homage to LA and undeniably Hockney—a playful sea of deep-blue, crescent-shaped strokes swimming across an olympic-sized cement canvas. Though this is not the artist's first such pool, it is his biggest, and since the others are at private homes, the only one open to

public viewing. Hollywood Roosevelt Hotel, 7000
Hollywood Boulevard; 466-7000.

4. Frank Gehry House Gehry's architectural
style can be seen and felt all over LA, starting with the
Loyola law school, spreading east to the Temporary
Contemporary, and west out to Rebecca's. His own
place—a once-bland, typical Santa Monica cottage—is a
tribute to the construction/design process: knocked-out
walls, altered rooms, and raised ceilings, all encased in a
shell of corrugated metal, plywood, glass, and chain link.
A must-see for students of architecture or an eyesore to
the neighborhood? You be the judge. 1002 22nd Street,
Santa Monica; private residence.

5. Gamble House The best known and best example
(all 8100 square feet of it) of the Craftsman-style bunga-
lows designed by architects and brothers Charles and
Henry Greene, this is the epitome of workmanship and
planning—from the cruciform structure of the living
room (which provides four distinctly separate areas for
entertaining) to the original furnishings and the strategi-
cally placed windows that create natural air-conditioning
by cross ventilation. Built in 1908 for the Gamble family
(as in Proctor & . . .) of Cincinnati, it is currently owned
by the USC School of Architecture, and tours are available. Living proof that there's more to LA houses than
push-button gas fireplaces and cottage cheese ceilings.
4 Westmoreland Place, Pasadena; (818) 793-3334.

6. The Hollywood Sign Originally the sign read
HOLLYWOODLAND and was constructed in 1923 as a hillside
advertisement to announce a new residential subdivision.
When the 50-foot-high letters began to deteriorate, the
Hollywood Chamber of Commerce took it over, dropped
the -LAND from the title, and a star was born. A drive
north on Gower will provide a good view from below; if
you want a close-up look, you'll have to park near Beech-
wood and Durand, then hike the hills a bit.

7. The Museum of Contemporary Art It's stretching
it to say that MOCA opened and—presto—LA ceased
to be thought of as a cultural wasteland. But the '84
Olympics aside, that could be just what happened.
Isozaki's building—an alluring combination of curves
and pyramids—certainly swept the art world off its feet.
A quick stroll through the series of skylit galleries and
you too will find it real hard not to be seduced. 250 S.
Grand Avenue, LA; 621-2766.

8. Pacific Design Center Six-hundred-feet long, its unmistakable outline overshadowing the small scale of the neighborhood, "The Blue Whale" was designed by Cesar Pelli in 1975 and functions as a wholesale mart (with a handful of retail outlets) to LA's decorators and interior designers. A second "mammal," a squarish green-glass addition with beveled and fluted walls, was opened in 1988, with a third red monster scheduled to follow by the early 1990s. 8687 Melrose Avenue, W. Hollywood; 675-0800.

9. Watts Towers The largest and possibly the most fantastic work of folk art in the world, "The Towers of Simon Rodia" (Attention Trivia Buffs: Rodia's first name was actually Sam; early news reports got it wrong and the artist, typically, never bothered to correct them) were 33 years in the making, constructed without plans, and the result of one man's dream "to build something great." And that he did. The frameworks (the tallest of which reaches 107 feet) are a conglomeration of salvaged mate-rials (metal rods, pieces of pipe, and old bed frames) that have been covered with tiny fragments of seashells, bottles, flower pots, ceramic tiles, and china plates. Extensive ren-ovation is badly needed; the towers have spent most of the last decade buried under scaffolding, their restoration lost in a web of internal wrangling and bureaucratic bull-shit. But while a fence surrounding the property keeps the public out, access to the interior is available during the occasional music festivals held on the grounds each year. 1765 E. 107th Street, Watts.

10. World's Oldest McDonald's If Los Angeles is the fast-food capital of the world, then this open-air time capsule should be City Hall. Purchased from the original McDonald brothers (for $2500, in 1953) before they sold out to Ray Kroc, it remains the only one of the 7600-plus in operation today that is independently owned. But be-cause it does not have to pay the corporation a franchise fee, what you're not going to find is Ronald McDonald, gimmicky decor, or any of those TV-advertised promo-tions. What you will find is vintage McDonald's architec-ture (from the rake of the roof down to the red-and-white-striped tile), outdoor seating only, old-fashioned cooking equipment (putting out McDonald's favorites, past and present) and the chain's original mascot: a winking, bun-faced chef named Speedee, who stands atop a 60-foot-high sign announcing "Your Kind of Place!" I couldn't have said it better. 10207 Lakewood, Downey; 869-6212.

Architectural Oddities

What you see is what you get. . . .

Photo Express One-stop sightseeing: first get the picture, then get it developed. 15336 Golden West Street, Westminster; (714) 897-4777.

Wigwam Village Motel Rooms run $35 a night. Scheduled for demolition in 1989, so call first. 2728 W. Foothill Boulevard, Rialto; (714) 875-0241.

Donut Hole It's traditional that newlyweds drive through it for good luck. On your way, try the "Mae West": a double-mounded donut in either chocolate or maple nut. 15300 E. Amar Road, La Puente; (818) 968-2912.

The Bear Tree Pure Pooh, with a touch of Laura Ashley. Teddy bears and collectibles in a tree-shaped store. 1240 S. Beach Boulevard, Anaheim; (714) 527-1411.

Tail o' the Pup An LA classic . . . the chili dog as well as the building. 329 N. San Vicente Boulevard, LA; 652-4517.

Culver City Historical Society Museum The famous Beverly Hills "Witch's House" has found a new home (and a new life as a museum) and by Summer 1989 will at last be open to the public. Culver City Park, corner Jefferson Boulevard at Duquesne Avenue.

Déjà View

Even to the first-time tourist, a drive through the streets of LA can seem strangely familiar. Exteriors of homes, offices, restaurants, churches, schools, and more are quickly recognizable, not for what they really are, but for the roles they've played on TV and in the movies.

City Hall Served double duty, as both police headquarters in *Dragnet* and as the *Daily Planet* building in the *Superman* TV series (remember when he flew around it in the opening credits?). Funny that a building so identifiable with LA is in fact modeled after the State Capitol in Nebraska. 200 N. Spring Street, Downtown.

USC/County General Millions of commuters pass it every day, not giving it a second thought, but to millions of others at home, the multi-winged, off-white building, behind the wrought-iron gates and up the steep drive, is clearly Port Charles's *General Hospital*. 1200 N. State Street, East LA.

UCLA Medical Center Not to be outdone by their cross-town college rival, UCLA lent their Medical Center (building, name, and all) to CBS so Chad Everett (as Joe Gannon) would have a place to practice weekly. Further north on the UCLA campus, Royce Hall is a star in its own right, having been featured prominently in *The Thorn Birds* and having played younger (as Walt Whitman High) in *Room 222*. Medical Center at 10833 Le Conte Avenue, Westwood.

Venice High School Also known as Rydell High, where Olivia Newton-John told John Travolta "You're the One That I Want" in *Grease*. 13000 Venice Boulevard, Venice.

All Saints Episcopal Church It was here that Dudley Moore saw Bo Derek for the first time (marrying the wrong man) in *10*. 504 N. Camden Drive, Beverly Hills.

United Methodist Church Sixties romantics cheered as Dustin Hoffman stormed the chapel, manned a crucifix, and rescued Katherine Ross in *The Graduate*. 3205 D Street, LaVerne.

Fox Plaza A typical Hollywood success story: With no previous experience, and despite serious competition, the new kid on the block gets tapped to co-star in a major motion picture. Could it have helped that the building was owned by a Fox affiliate and that the film was produced for Twentieth Century? Even so, it managed to hold its own opposite leading man Bruce Willis, as the high-rise taken hostage in *Die Hard*. 2121 Avenue of the Stars, Century City.

Chez Denis Chez Denis is currently boarded up and closed, but 30 years ago this restaurant was known as "Dino's Lodge" (in reality it was owned by Dean Martin), and when it wasn't serving dinner it was serving as the spot—*77 Sunset Strip*—where "Kookie" was parking cars and lending girls his comb. 8524 W. Sunset Boulevard, W. Hollywood.

From the Cast-Your-Own-Couch Department: Only in LA do houses have agents. If you think your home (or store, office, or apartment building) has star potential, both *Media Locations* (559-5545) and *Reel to Reel* (461-0038) can help in bringing property owners and production companies together.

The Source The parking lot has been paved and the front patio fenced in, but you can still get sprouts and veggie burgers here, and it's still the place where Diane Keaton told Woody Allen good-bye in *Annie Hall*. 830 W. Sunset Boulevard, W. Hollywood.

Los Angeles State and County Arboretum One hundred-twenty-seven acres of lush greenery, rose gardens, waterfalls, and fountains does make this park seem like paradise, so it is only fitting that it was in front of the 1886 Victorian-style Queen Anne Cottage situated here that Mr. Roarke and Tatoo welcomed their guests to *Fantasy Island*. 301 N. Baldwin Avenue, Arcadia.

750 Bel Air Road, Bel Air (private residence) Back in 1962, a family from the Ozarks struck it rich, loaded up their truck, and moved to Beverly Hills. While this address is actually Bel Air, and the swimming pool on the property is not the famous "cement pond," the long drive and impressive exterior did stand in as the new digs for Jed, Granny, and the rest of *The Beverly Hillbillies*.

565 N. Cahuenga Avenue (private residence) This very midwestern, white wooden house looks like it belongs to the all-American family (which makes it totally out of place in LA), and for 11 years it did—as the Cunningham home on *Happy Days*.

1145 Arden, Pasadena (private residence) The house pictured in the opening credits of *Dynasty* is, obviously, in Denver. But portions of this house and the surrounding grounds have stood in as the Carrington home for the entire run of the series. And they've got the infamous lily pond, where Krystle and Alexis slugged it out, to prove it.

160 San Rafael, Pasadena (private residence) Holy Real Estate! Pasadena sure isn't Gotham City, but this is definitely the mansion where Bruce Wayne, a.k.a. *Batman*, and his youthful ward Dick Grayson secretly transformed themselves into The Dynamic Duo to rid the world (Zap! Pow! Bam!) of crime and corruption.

Gamble House Not just another LA landmark (see "Ten Sites and Structures that Capture the City's Lifestyle") but also the home where Michael J. Fox tracked down Christopher Lloyd and his time-traveling DeLorean to help him get *Back to the Future*. 4 Westmoreland Place, Pasadena.

927 Vendome, Silverlake Ignore the building and check out the stairway on the side. It was here in 1932 that Laurel and Hardy made *The Music Box*—and made movie history—in a scene where they attempted to deliver a piano to the top.

B

"I don't know, Marty, what do you want to do?"

Unique Answers to that Age-Old Question

5

The Best Cheap Dates in LA

We name names. . . .

Date #1: Box Seats at the Bowl

Cost: Free. *Details:* Okay, so you won't be going at night. And you'll be drinking coffee and munching donuts (which you've brought along, by the way) instead of sipping champagne and nibbling caviar. You see, on Tuesday, Thursday, and Friday mornings, rehearsals for that evening's performance are in full swing and open to the public. Same program, no charge. No fireworks, either. But you won't care. The music and the atmosphere are LA's premiere class act . . . even at 9 A.M. **Hollywood Bowl,** 2301 N. Highland Avenue, Hollywood; 850-2000.

Date #2: Dinner and a Movie

Cost: $10 for two (including popcorn). *Details:* Once a cheap date staple, it's gotten to the point that going to the movies (let alone then going out to dinner) can mean a second mortgage. But not so at the **Rainbow Theater.** On any night, $2 buys you a first-run double (sometimes triple) feature except, that is, on Tuesdays, when a mind-boggling 75¢ will get you in. And once inside, the bargains keep on coming: the grill at the Rainbow Broiler Hut serves up a pretty decent deluxe burger—along with fries and something to drink—for the same as what you'd pay for a box of Jujubes in Westwood. 6721 Foothill Boulevard, Tujunga; (818) 353-8505.

The slightly more flush might opt to hit the **Vista Theater** ($3 for a double bill), then dash down the street to eat at nearby **Seafood Bay.** Reminiscent of a classic New England seafood joint (a smattering of tables, a service counter selling fresh fish, and a line spilling down the block), it promises one of the best bargain meals in town: shrimp, salmon, swordfish, soft shell crabs, and more, at an average price of $6.95. A la carte? No way. You get hunks of sourdough bread and your choice of two from the following: whole sauteed mushrooms, rice pilaf, house potatoes, sliced tomatos, and fresh veggies. Tartar sauce is homemade. On Sundays, when the restaurant is closed, the owner goes fishing around the Channel Islands. If the catch is good, expect to see it offered on Monday's menu. Vista Theater, 4473 Sunset Drive, E. Hollywood; 660-6639. Seafood Bay, 3916 Sunset Boulevard, Silverlake; 664-3902; also at 1240 S. Soto, LA; 269-6874.

Cost: $10 to $20 for two. *Details:* All dressed up with no place to go and less than $20 to go there? Then head downtown to Rex. Forget that you can't remember a restaurant more visually spectacular anywhere else. (Designed to resemble a '30s luxury liner, this one's the essence of style and glamour.) Just trust me.

Needless to say, you'll have to forgo eating. Beauty doesn't come cheap, especially on the first floor. But follow the sweeping stairway to the mezzanine piano bar; it will not disappoint. How could it, with its black marble floor, backlit Lalique ceiling, streamlined steel, and romantic view of the city? Strains of Cole Porter fill the air. Anything goes. Settle into a plush, peach sofa and place your order. "Vodka martini, extra dry, two olives . . ." Glide across the tiny dance floor, recalling Fred and Ginger. And gloat. While the folks downstairs shell out $150 plus to soak up all this grandeur, for the price of a single drink ($5 to $9), the same world is yours. **Rex il Ristorante,** 617 S. Olive Street, Downtown; 627-2300.

**Date #3:
Out Together
Dancing Cheek-
to-Cheek**

Cost: $10 per person (depending what you eat or drink). *Details:* Let the good times roll. With cheap food (everything from sushi to jambalaya, depending on where you go), cheaper drinks (figure $1.50 for a Corona), late hours (weekends till 3 A.M.) and no cover, it's no wonder that going bowling has become as popular as going to a club. And why not? Low costs aside, it's relaxing, sociable, a feasible way to get a good-size group together, and just retro enough to be in. So in, in fact, that some alley owners have sat up and taken notice. Friday nights at Studio City's **Sports Center** now feature "Moonlight Madness," where from midnight to three in the morning, the lights are turned down, rock 'n roll is cranked up, and $7 buys all you can bowl. . . . Similarly, "Rockin' Bowl" at **Westminster Lanes** (Fridays and Saturdays, 11:30 P.M. to 4 A.M.) is also packing them in. An added bonus: Score a strike and you possibly score free albums or concert tickets. Sports Center, 12655 Ventura Boulevard, Studio City; (818) 769-7600. Westminster Lanes, 6451 Westminster Avenue, Westminster; (714) 893-5005.
Sushi and sake available at **Tokyo Bowl,** Yohan Square, 333 S. Alameda Street, Downtown; 626-7376.
Jambalaya and cajun/creole/southern food available at **Cafe Beignet**, Bayshore Bowl, 234 Pico Boulevard, Santa Monica; 399-7731.

**Date #4: Late-
Night Fun**

Date #5:
Art and
Entertainment

Cost: $15 to $20 for two. *Details:* Paint the town red without using a lot of green. Your first stop: **Yee Mee Loo,** one of Chinatown's few bars and a throwback to 1940. The feeling is Raymond Chandler, the jukebox plays Sinatra, and whiskey runs two bucks a shot. Next, catch the latest exhibits on view at **MOCA** and the **Temporary Contemporary,** both open late on Thursdays and Fridays, and both free of charge from 5 to 8 P.M. Then move on to dinner at **Gorky's,** the aptly named Russian cafe, where the food is great, the prices better (figure $7 per) and the beer brewed on the premises. Eating here is actually two cheap dates in one, with live jazz, swing, or rockabilly happening each night after nine. Until then, you should just kick back and watch the people, an endless stream of poets, MBA candidates, actor-types with ponytails, and 80-year-old men playing chess. The atmosphere? Art school cafeteria. And since the set-up is self-serve, you won't have to deal with a waitress standing over, shooting you looks for tying up her table. Just your own guilty conscience when you eye the line at the door.

Yee Mee Loo, 690 N. Spring Street, Chinatown; 624-4539. Museum of Contemporary Art (250 S. Grand)/Temporary Contemporary (152 N. Central), Downtown; 626-6222. Gorky's Cafe, 536 E. Eighth Street, Downtown; 627-4060.

Date #6:
Hanging Out

Cost: $10 for two. *Details:* It's just after 9 P.M. What you'd like is a place where you can sit and talk, linger over coffee, and maybe get something to eat. But you don't want a four-course meal, so most restaurants don't want you. Your favorite burger and pie joint is nothing but stools at a counter. The cafe would be perfect, except the seats are made for people with cheeks the size of Cher's. And the deli closes at ten. All of which means a good hangout is hard to find.

Make that *was.* At **Gasoline Alley**, there's an espresso machine working overtime, dozens of decent desserts, and a stack of games on the bar. The decor has all the charm of a Sunday-school basement, but there's something refreshing about a prime Melrose location with not a speck of faux marble in sight. At a front table, a frenetic game of Pictionary is going on; over in the corner, a couple sits oblivious, their heads buried in books. Owners Sharyn Rubenstein and Victor Puca deserve a medal. Here at last, LA, is a neighborhood coffeehouse; a place devoted to hanging around and hanging out, where a bottomless cuppa java is a dollar and desserts ($3.50) are as good and basic as what Aunt Bessie used to bake. You'll find salads and sandwiches as well, but no stigma to spending just a little—and then spending all night at a table. That's what it's all about. 7219 Melrose Avenue, LA; 937-5177.

6

The Best Ways and Means to Celebrate a Special Occasion

*It used to be that going out to dinner was
something special. You only did it
to celebrate a birthday or any other big
event. But today, with two-career marriages
the norm—and trying new restaurants a
barometer of hipness—it's really no big deal.
Fact is, one out of every two meals is eaten out.*

*So to put the happy back in birthday, a
number of unusual dining experiences are
cropping up all across LA. Say goodbye to
that quiet little table in the corner. Because
now, when you go out to dinner, you can
go way out. . . .*

A quick drive down the 405 and you'll feel like you're in
Italy. All it takes is a loaf of bread, a jug of wine, and of
course, a gondola. **Gondola Getaways** (433-9595)
offers romantic rides through the century-old Long Beach
harbors and canals. While the 30-foot Caorlina carries up
to 14 people and has been used for full-blown dinner parties afloat, it is the smaller vessels (perfect for two and
stocked with glasses, ice bucket, and a basket of bread,
cheese, and salami) that will have you singing arias. It's
amore, all right, and it's available any day of the year, any
time of day, from sunrise to midnight, with prices starting
around $45.

To most people, picnicking can be a hassle; first, with the
long trek to escape the city, then getting there and meeting up with the hoards of other people who've escaped
the same as you. Though primarily designed to service
weddings, **Barton's Horse-Drawn Carriages**
(818-447-6693) can make picnicking a pleasure. It all starts
with a serene ride in your choice of any of their 15 antique
carriages—from open buggy and glass coach to a surrey
with the fringe on top. Then lean back and enjoy. With
18 years experience, there are few city streets the horse
(always white, by the way) and the driver (formally
attired) cannot handle. Detour through the LA Arboretum
or the Pasadena Arroyo, taking in the scenery, but primarily just wowing the people you pass by. Hungry? Stop in a
nearby orchard or secluded grassy meadow. What you eat

is up to you, since it's up to you to bring the food. Just time it so you don't finish before sundown; if it's dark, they decorate the horse and carriage with over 200 tiny white lights to see you home.

Horses at twilight are also an integral part of the glorious moonlit ride at Hollywood's **Sunset Ranch** (3400 N. Beachwood Drive, Hollywood; 469-5450). Join the weekly Friday night dinner trip ($25, plus food) or schedule one of your own (you'll need a minimum of 15 people). Either way, you'll start at dusk, ride for almost two hours over the hills into the Valley (the view is stupendous), have dinner at a Mexican restaurant (mediocre, so settle for margaritas instead), and head back by the light of the moon. Later, should you want a bite to eat, you should stop at the cozy **Cafe des Artistes** (see "Best Little-Known Sunday Brunch"), where you can snuggle on the outdoor patio, count the stars and toast another year. . . .

Dreams Come True (661-1300; see "Made to Order: A Catalog of Uniquely Personal Gifts") will also fulfill anybody's birthday dinner fantasies, arranging catered meals (and more) in a range of luxurious locales: on a private stretch of beach, atop a downtown skyscraper, or simply served in bed. Their only limitation is your imagination, and of course, your budget.

For folks with a sense of adventure, **Ultimate Dimensions in Dining** (818-349-1895) could be the answer. Owner Bill McColloch plans progressive dinner parties, hauling guests around in a cushy chartered coach for a night of non-stop table hopping. It all starts with waiters serving champagne and hors d'oeuvres on board, then proceeds to appetizers, entrees, and, desserts. The fun, of course, is that each course is eaten at a different restaurant, and McColloch's choices are as inspired as they are tasteful.

But what about those times—a 50th anniversary or a 60th birthday, for example—when, with 100 or so guests, only a boring banquet room will do? (Hold on. See "Private Rooms for Private Parties"). Whatever you decide, **Nostalgia Productions** (277-5865) can add just the touch of class you need, expertly putting together a video documentary that celebrates your family's history. Material is culled from home movies, photo albums, yearbooks, and the like, then intercut with stock footage, taped

Gondolas don't interest you. Horse-drawn carriages seem extreme. And you could care less about how good or bad the food is. The point is, you've picked the place you want to go because it holds sentimental value. Okay, I give. But if dinner looks like it is going to be ordinary, then why not make the ride there something special? **London Taxi Ltd.** (818-716-0556) offers a fleet of beautifully refurbished, chauffeur-driven Austins, perfect for being toted around town in grand and proper style. Rates are comparable to standard limo companies ($40 an hour), with point-to- point fares available on short trips and airport runs. Good show!

interviews with relatives and friends, and music of the era. Finally, a specially written narration is added, designed to bring the insight and reflections of the present to the images of your past. The result is a lasting piece of quality filmmaking, done with humor and great warmth.

The Best Ways to Spend a Sunny Sunday in LA

7

Al Bussell Ranch A family-run farm with 200 acres of fruits and vegetables grown strictly for folks who want to pick their own. More than 145 different varieties are available between April and October: your choice of berries, peaches, plums, apples, melons, corn, tomatos . . . the list is endless. Free samples of whatever is in season are offered in the Country Store, enabling you to try and taste before you go and pick. You'll also find abundant picnic areas plus a farm animal exhibit, visible bee hive, and hay maze for the kids. 26500 Stockdale Highway, Bakersfield; (805) 589-2324.

Good Pickins

Outdoor Antique and Collectible Market The biggest, the best, and the most fun. Held the third Sunday of every month (they also stage a yearly Holiday Show, usually the first Sunday in November), it features over 600 exhibitors. Unlike the flea markets and swap meets, there is no new merchandise here. The stock ranges from priceless items to pieces in desperate need of restoration, and you're sure to find it all: furniture, collectibles (a favorite stall sells nothing but salt-and-pepper shakers), even antique cars. Admission: $2.50. Long Beach Veterans Memorial Stadium, Lakewood Boulevard at Conant Street, Long Beach; 655-5703.

Good and Plenty

"Babes in the Woods" A blessing for new parents feeling housebound. Designed for infants and kids up to age three, this is a stroller accessible hike, where mommies and daddies are more than welcome to tag along. Docents lead the way through Franklin Canyon Reservoir, pointing things out in a way that kids can understand, getting them to smell sage leaves or search for bird tracks as they go. There's no fee, but reservations are required. Additional programs include "Babes at the Beach" (a wade through the Malibu Lagoon), "Tykes on Hikes" (a nature walk for ages four to six), and "Tales in the Woods," a story-telling hour that focuses on local legends, Indian lore, and animal fables. William O. Douglas Outdoor Classroom; 858-3834.

Good (Quality) Time

Good Company

Angels Attic If you can't spend Sunday at Grandma's, this could be the next best thing: a spectacular dollhouse and miniature museum, tucked away in a beautifully restored 19th-century Victorian home. The displays, which also include antique dolls, model trains, and toys, are great fun; their intricacy and craftsmanship amazing. Finish off your visit in classic small-town style, with afternoon tea, lemonade, and cookies on the front porch. Admission: $3 for adults, $2 for seniors, and $1 for kids under 12. 516 Colorado Avenue, Santa Monica; 394-8331.

Good Going

Bird's Nest Off you go into the wild blue yonder. Bertie Duffy will see to it that you spend your Sunday flying high, taking you on an adventurous ride in a WWII open-cockpit bi-plane. Relive the glory: she'll supply you with helmet and goggles; all you need is the scarf. Prices: $75 to $125, the latter buying an hour-long ride from Hollywood to the beach. Contact (818) 785-5297.

Good Growing

Rancho Santa Ana Botanic Garden Botanic gardens are not uncommon in LA, from the Arboretum to the majestic grounds around the Huntington Library. RSA is unique because its 35 acres contain only local flora. You'll find 1550 plant species indigenous to California; cool cactus, too. 1500 N. College, Claremont; (714) 625-8767.

Good Clean Fun

Wheeler Hot Springs An eight-hour vacation. Start with a soak in the hot tubs (filled with water from the springs), enjoy a "spa cuisine" brunch on the outdoor patio, then spend the afternoon letting them massage your cares away. Tubs: $7.50/half hour. Massage: $30 to $65. Special hot tub and brunch for two, $36. Highway 33, Ojai; (805) 646-8131.

Glen Ivy Hot Springs A resort hotel without the hotel—"Club Mud." You can pamper yourself silly, be it in mud and hot mineral baths or in the Italian-tiled pools surrounding an outdoor stage. The live concerts range from reggae to Vivaldi. Prices are $12.50 weekdays, $14.75 weekends. Off Interstate 5, Corona; (714) 737-4723.

Good for You

UCLA Franklin Murphy Sculpture Gardens On Sundays, the campus is quiet and the sculpture gardens pleasantly deserted. It's just you, lots of green, and an incomparable collection of Miró, Rodin, Matisse, Moore, and Noguchi. You could bring a friend and a picnic basket if you wanted. But I can think of no better place to go alone, just to sit and read the Sunday paper. Especially in April, when the jacarandas are in bloom. UCLA Campus (use Hilgard entrance), Westwood; 825-4321.

As the day starts to fade, drive north on Pacific Coast Highway, passing Malibu Canyon Road. Turn right on Corral Canyon, following it up, toward the hills. When the road stops, get out and hike up to the top. It's all dry earth and boulders where you're standing, but like they say, on a clear day. . . . You'll have a 360-degree panorama of the city, from the Pacific Coast to the west Valley to downtown. And what a sight as the sun sets on it all.

Sunset Ranch See "The Best Ways and Means to Celebrate a Special Occasion."

See also "A Guide to Unusual Guided Tours" and "The Best Sunday Brunch/The Best Little-Known Sunday Brunch."

Good Night (or the Best Way to End a Sunny Sunday in LA)

Mentioned Elsewhere

8

24-Hour LA

All-Night Snacking

Finding a donut at four in the morning is hardly a problem; feeling unsatisfied three stale bear claws later is. So forego the convenient and head instead to **Western Bagel** (7814 N. Sepulveda, Van Nuys; 818-786-5847), where one whiff tells you there isn't a frozen, pre-packaged, or day-old good in sight. Western's bakery supplies to numerous restaurants, delis, and supermarket chains in town, turning out 18 varieties (the usuals, plus pizza, jalapeno, and blueberry) as well as a selection of six flavored-cream cheese spreads. Try the cinnamon—topped with honey-nut-and-raisin—and you'll never look twice at a Winchell's again.

All-Night Dining

When eating late means really late, then clearly the destination of choice is downtown. It's no secret that **Gorky's, The Pantry,** and **The Pacific Dining Car** are all open 'round the clock, any one of them guaranteed to feed you well. But knowledgeable all-night noshers also flock to the **Flower Market Restaurant** (765 Wall Street; 623-4323). Forget that a place that closes by early afternoon is listed under a "24-hour" heading; it's the fact that they *open* at 3 A.M. that matters. Like the better known (and no less wonderful) **Vickman's,** the odd schedule is designed to accommodate the workers from the nearby produce and floral marts, while the off-beat menu (a blend of traditional coffee-shop fare with some really decent Chinese food) will please even the pickiest nocturnal palate.

If romance is on your mind, however, then about face, young man (or woman), and go west to watch the sun rise, stopping first to share an old-fashioned ice cream soda (or to split the red-eye special) at either **Edie's Diner** (4211 Admiralty Way, Marina del Rey; 823-5339) or **Bennie the Bum's** (238 Laguna Avenue, Laguna Beach; 714-497-4786). Not only do both dish out edible Americana in retro '50s settings, but they do it night and day and in locations just a block or two from the beach. For those who balk at eating late on the theory that it can't be good for them, **I Love Juicy** (7174 Melrose Avenue, LA; 935-7247) is a 24-hour vegetarian restaurant (probably the world's only one). Polish off one of the tasteless tofu dishes and seconds later you'll be asking "Have we eaten yet?" but the veggie platters are good, the tabbouleh excellent, and the 15 varieties of juices fresh and squeezed to order.

On the other hand, **Belisle's** (12001 Harbor Boulevard, Garden Grove; 714-750-6560) is synonymous with serious wee-hour chowing down—a bustling family restaurant where size definitely makes a difference. The legendary "Texas Breakfast" consists of juice, a 26-ounce sirloin, 12 eggs any style, a stack of hot cakes, home fries, plus biscuits, corn bread, or toast. Lunch and dinner are no small potatoes either, with salads that could feed a family of four, sandwiches piled perilously high, cuts of meat bigger than the platters that carry them, and iced tea in quart-sized glasses. Ask for dessert and they'll bring you the whole cake.

All-Night Exercise

Still, no need to wake up feeling guilty about what you did the night before. Though you'll be hard-pressed to find an aerobics class scheduled later than 9 P.M., the weight rooms at **Beverly Hills Health and Fitness** (8301 Beverly Boulevard, LA; 658-6999)—as well as those at selected branches of the **Nautilus Plus** clubs—are ready and waiting anytime, making it possible to go work out before you go to bed. . . . But it's far more fun (and currently more cool) to burn the calories bowling. **Mar Vista Bowl** (12125 Venice Boulevard, Mar Vista; 391-4588) is the kingpin of the all-night alleys (albeit Thursdays to Saturdays only), offering 28 lanes, automatic scoring, and overhead TV monitors that shamelessly announce your every strike, spare, or gutterball. . . . And should that late date leave you in the mood for love, the **Merchant of Tennis** (1118 S. La Cienega Boulevard, LA; 855-1946) has two concrete courts available, all night as well as day. Be advised that you will have to take precautions, as reservations must be made in advance, during store hours.

All-Night Services

Pharmacy: **Horton and Converse,** 6625 Van Nuys Boulevard, Van Nuys; 818-782-6251.

Newsstand: **World Book & News,** 1652 Cahuenga Boulevard, Hollywood; 465-4352.

Dry Cleaners: **Studio Cleaners** (Monday–Friday only), 10800 Washington Boulevard, Culver City; 838-1801.

Laundromat: **Blue Ribbon Wash and Dry,** 2081 Hillhurst Avenue, Los Feliz.

Xeroxing: **Copy Mat,** 6301 Sunset Boulevard, Hollywood; 461-1222.

Car Repairs: **A-1 Automotive** The theory here is that at 3 A.M., even a small problem is a big problem. But be warned: the two mechanics who are on duty nightly will only deal with one- to two-hour jobs; for a major overhaul, you'll still have to wait until morning. 4430 Santa Monica Boulevard, Hollywood; 661-5352.

Almost All Night, but Not Quite

Heading the list is the **LA Flower Mart,** where the florists who sell the stuff go to buy it. You'll find exotic blooms from midnight *till* dawn, at wholesale prices yet, with the trendiest stems at Tayama (627-3473). 754 Wall Street, Downtown.

Used to be you couldn't sleep, you got up and read a book; nowadays, more and more insomniacs are choosing movies. While lots of 7–Elevens offer all-night rental service, your choice is pretty much limited to *Care Bears* and teen comedies. Better to check out **Video Ga Ga** (8932 Santa Monica Boulevard, W. Hollywood; 659- 0962). The hours aren't as good (they close at 3 A.M.), but the selection runs the entire film-buff gambit, from *Billboard*'s Top Twenty to cult, classic, and foreign.

Mentioned Elsewhere

Residential Services See "House Callers."

Unusual Classes, Courses, and Clubs

9

Gumshoe 101

According to publishers, one out of every four fiction books sold is a mystery or suspense novel. But why simply remain an armchair detective? The **Nick Harris Detective Academy** (818-981-9911) has been turning out wannabe PIs since 1907, with job placement upon graduation a virtual guarantee. Who's done it? Everyone from truck drivers to grandmothers to law school graduates. Tuition for the seven-week course is $3500 (hey, they mean business), with licensed detectives, policemen, and fire captains teaching classes on surveillance, debugging, undercover work, fingerprinting, arson, and more.

Magic Close-Up

This is the real stuff, not the kind of tricks you learned in cub scouts. Magician **Jim Kalhert** (472-3770) is a performer at the Magic Castle and a veteran of the corporate trade-show circuit. In a series of six easy lessons, he'll show you all the basics to working with cards, coins, scarves, and ropes. Amuse your family! Amaze your friends!

Introduction to Witchcraft

Everything you wanted to know about tarot, numerology, ceremonial magic, alchemy, and voodoo, but were too superstitious to ask. The six-week classes, offered by the **Sorcerer's Shop** (656-1563), include a seminar with a Native American medicine man and lectures from guest authors.

Things Are Really Cooking

And with over three dozen LA-area businesses offering culinary classes, it's no wonder. Each scores high marks, but hard-core foodies rank **Epicurean** (8759 Melrose Avenue, W. Hollywood; 659-5990) number one. With an extensive three-month program for the would-be professional, hands-on workshops taught by big-name chefs, a "Kids' Kitchen Kamp," and seminars on starting your own catering company or opening a small restaurant successfully, you'd be hard-pressed to find a better range of courses.

An A for originality goes to **Culinary Adventures** (456-2484), a self-labeled "classroom on wheels" that schedules day-long, food-related field trips. A trip up the Southern California "Gold Coast," for example, starts with a continental breakfast, followed by a visit to a fig-tree ranch in Malibu, then a tour of a plant that supplies gourmet lettuces to restaurants (buying is permitted, at well-below-wholesale prices), a stop at a top-of-the-line roadside produce stand, and a catered picnic at an Ojai Ranch (where the fruit trees are ripe for the picking). And that's only the beginning: there's also a sausage-making demo, a look at a banana plantation, and a wine-tasting seminar to help you wash it all down.

I'd Rather Be Eating

Leave the cooking to someone else. The same folks responsible for LA a la Carte and the Foodsource Hot-line have organized **The Gourmet Dinner Club** (930-0893), bringing together individuals anxious to try new as well as undiscovered restaurants all over town. Events accommodate from 40 to 100 people, and cover a wide range of cuisines, locations, and prices.

Will You Still Need Me, Will You Still Feed Me, When I'm Sixty-Four?

For LA's seniors, **Grand People's Company** (290 S. Garey Street, LA; 680-4311) makes the question obsolete. Since 1981, this non-profit organization has offered an ongoing series of programs for persons 55 and older, be it twilight cabarets or all-day excursions to local museums, beaches, and public gardens. (They even arrange several on-bus-only tours, geared towards those in wheelchairs and with walkers.). Their Grand People's Breakfast Club features top Hollywood entertainment (past guests include Eve Arden, Milton Berle, Ruby Keeler, Dom DeLuise, and Alice Faye), along with former Ziegfeld girls, Mack Sennett bathing beauties, and veteran stage performers. And not only do they do this 20 to 30 times a year, but, like everything else, they do it free of charge, with bus transportation to and from provided.

What's Your Cause?

Singles fed up with having to endure yet another wine-and-cheese affair should check out **LA CAN** (459-4665). CAN stands for Community Action Network, appropriate because the basis for the group is volunteer work, whether it's visiting an area nursing home or staffing the Special Olympics. And nice, because what results is an easy, casual, non-threatening way to meet new people. Who knows if a lasting relationship will come of it, but at least you won't walk away feeling that the day was a total waste.

It's in Their Blood

Calling all horror fans: the **Count Dracula Society** (752-5811) wants you. Open to anyone who loves scary books, plays, and movies, this 27-year-old organization holds meetings once a month. Scheduled events range from panel discussions and guest lecturers to film screenings and an annual awards dinner, where foot-tall Dracula statuettes are presented to the likes of Ray Bradbury and Christopher Lee.

Great Camps and Programs for Kids

Young Professionals' Company An extensive program taught by professionals that covers every aspect of working in the theater. Kids (ages six to sixteen) not only star in an original production, but (with the exception of an adult director), take on all of the backstage roles as well. Though admission to the company is through audition, selection is equally based on commitment, enthusiasm, interest, and talent. Santa Monica Playhouse; 394-9779.

Should the acting bug keep biting them, however, check in with **Center Stage LA** (837-4536), where owner/teacher Kevin McDermott runs comedy improv classes specifically for teens. . . . Or check out the 12-week session at Diane Hardin's **Young Actors' Space** (818-785-7979), certainly the most intensive workshop for kids in town, and with classes involving theater games, memorized scene work, and monologues. Reputed to be one of the best.

Catalina Sea Camp A year-round, overnight marine biology camp for grades 3 and up, with one- and three-week sessions scheduled during the summer, and 3-to-5-day programs planned for the remainder of the year. Activities range from swimming and fishing to snorkeling and diving, with touch tank and astronomy set-ups also available. Catalina Island Marine Institute; 510-1622. . . . Should your kid wish to stay closer to home, **Oceanic Society Sea Camp,** (Chase Park, Marina del Rey; 393-3776) offers a similar-style program, but as a series of daily field trips. In any given week, they'll explore tide pools, wade through Malibu Lagoon, dig for fossils, tour a marine science lab, and ride on a Coast Guard cutter.

Zoo Camp A traditional day camp, made special due to the unique setting. One-week sessions only, which are limited to ages 8 to 11. Your budding Jane Goodalls and Dian Fosseys will love it. Los Angeles Zoo; 664-1100.

Olympic Boys and Girls Club A sports-only day camp for ages 6 to 14, with excellent instruction in basketball, baseball, swimming, tennis, soccer . . . you name it, they do it. Merrie Anderson, owner; 477-6864.

Inside LA An imaginative series of guided tours—scheduled throughout the year, but predominantly in summer—that gives kids an insider's look at places they normally don't get to go to. The itinerary changes, but usually includes hands-on visits to artists' studios, trips through factories churning out everything from glass to billboard signs to tortilla chips, and a behind-the-scenes peek at the audio-animatronic division of Disney. The favorite? A midnight journey through LA after dark, ending with breakfast at 3 A.M. and a sleepover at the museum. (Offered through the Los Angeles Children's Museum; 687-8226.

Valley Student Tours A six-week, co-ed teen-tour program that takes high school students cross-country to historical locations, national parks, and major cities such as New York, D.C., Boston, Chicago, Philadelphia, New Orleans, and Quebec. Stops to check out numerous colleges and universities are also scheduled along the way; academic credit in U.S. history, government, or social studies can be arranged. Summer school never sounded so good. Ann and Coach Bill Brown; (818) 247-7717.

UC Family Camps Who said that kids had to be the only ones to have all the summer fun? The University of California offers week-long camps (in three locations, no less) designed for the entire family to enjoy together. While you need not be an alumnus, you do need to be a member of the Alumni Association, but joining is easy and fairly inexpensive. For more information, call 825-3901. For Bruin Woods in Lake Arrowhead, (714) 337-2478; for UC Santa Barbara Camp, (805)961-3123; for Lair of the Bear in Yosemite, (415) 642-0221.

Get Away Without Going Away

10

Great vacations at home
(because 50 million tourists
can't be wrong)

Kick Back . . .

Ask just about anyone where they'd most like to spend a weekend and they're likely to tell you "the beach." **The Venice Beach House** isn't *on* the beach, but it is at the beach; and while steps away from the sand, it's a world apart from all the hustle and bustle. This is overstuffed country comfort in a beautifully restored 1911 seaside craftsman home. The nine guest rooms range in price from $50 to $150: Cora's Corner ($90), all peach with antique white wicker (and a canopied iron bed), so impressed an executive from Mattel that it became the model for Barbie's Dream House. The Pier Suite ($150) features a fireplace, separate sitting area, and ocean view; done in grays and mauves, its contemporary furnishings are a welcomed contrast to the cutesy calico or Laura Ashley look you tend to associate with bed and breakfasts. Reduced midweek rates available. 15 30th Avenue, Venice; 823-1966.

Relax . . .

A weekend escape to the Valley might sound like someone's idea of a joke, and a drive through the endless line of tire dealers and taco stands should give you little reason to expect any different. But suddenly—unexpectedly—a gracious Italian villa rises up on a quiet North Hollywood street. Welcome to **La Maida House,** once a rancher's mansion, more recently a rundown retirement home, and now the grande dame of LA's bed and breakfast elite. And with good reason: it's hard to imagine another place in the city more private, perfect, or conducive for holing up and doing nothing. There are 12 large rooms and suites (ranging from $85 to $210), some with full kitchens, private patios, and fireplaces; others with bathrooms big enough to get lost in. The grounds are no less spectacular, complete with rose bushes, flower gardens, swimming pool, swan pond, fruit trees, and towering magnolias. Relax in the solarium, work out in the gymnasium, enjoy breakfast (eggs straight from their own chickens) on the outside terrace. Owner Megan Timothy is an award-winning chef, and with advance notice, will also prepare picnic baskets, pretheater suppers, and elaborate four-course gourmet

dinners. Life here should be the norm. 11159 La Maida
Street, N. Hollywood; (818) 769-3857.

Take Your Shoes Off

It's no secret that early morning at Grand Central Market
to after hours at The Second Coming, downtown LA is
ripe for rediscovery. It's lesser known that many of the
city's best hotels, because they cater to the weekday business set, sit virtually empty on the weekends. So to fill
these rooms, a lot of them, including the charming
Eastlake Inn (1442 Kellam Avenue, Angelino Heights;
250-1620; see "Wanted: A Great Spot to Tie the Knot") and
the magnificently restored **Biltmore**, (515 S. Olive
Street, Downtown; 624-1011) are offering elaborate pack-
age deals or special Saturday prices. While not exactly
cheap ($379 for two, tax and tips included), the "Japanese
Experience" at **The New Otani** (120 S. Los Angeles
Street, Downtown; 629-1200) makes a ritual of rest and
relaxation: sake on arrival, a wonderful tatami suite (with
futon beds, shoji screens, and sunken tub), an hour-long
shiatsu massage (as well as spa and sauna), dinner at A
Thousand Cranes (the best tempura in town, by the way),
breakfast from room service, and a *yukata* (cotton robe)
to wrap yourself in and take home.

And Make Yourself at Home

But why limit your getaway to a conventional hotel, an
inn, or even a B&B? **California Houseguests
International** specializes in alternative accommoda-
tions, in a wide range of rates and locations. Would you
believe the upper floor of a chalet in Malibu, with a separate entrance and an ocean view? A private guest house
high in the hills, surrounded by gardens and a gazebo? A
houseboat at the Marina? An artist's loft? Or renovated
servants' quarters on a suburban ranch, with tennis
courts, swimming pool, and an owner who's a gourmet
cook? All are available and many run well under $100 a
night, making it possible not only to get away, but to do it
without going broke. 18653 Ventura Boulevard, Suite
190-B, Tarzana; (818) 344-7878.

When You Absolutely, Positively Have to Get Out of Town

Going away is one thing; getting there is another. So the
next time you're ready to fly off into the sunset, rather
than book a reservation, why not book a gig as a courier
instead? Forget what you've seen in the movies. It isn't
that exciting. What is, however, is that you'll get to travel
for practically next to nothing.

Unlike Federal Express, Emory, or Purolator, smaller courier companies do not own their own planes. Instead they buy tickets on commercial carriers (say, United) and then check the packages they need to send as baggage. Since the baggage claim checks must get from LA to the agent awaiting pickup on the other end, someone has to carry them. Someone has to take that flight. A simple phone call, and that someone could be you.

On Board Courier (P.O. Box 92840, LA 90009; 642-7774) runs round trips to New York, Honolulu, and Chicago, as well as flights between San Francisco and New York, and is one of several companies that, for a nominal fee, will sell you their ticketed seats ($50 to $75, one way, depending on the city and the season). The only restrictions are that you be 18 years of age and that your luggage be limited to two carry-on bags. There's no catch, nothing illegal going on, and good or bad, you'll be treated the same as any other passenger.

IBC (8825-C S. Sepulveda, LA 90045; 216-1637) also arranges courier flights departing from LA—domestically to Miami ($50 one way), but primarily to Sydney, Australia, as well as Singapore, Hong Kong, Tokyo, and Taiwan. (Round-trip rates start as low as $250.) While the prices are unbeatable, they do require that their couriers be 21 and, on international flights, that they post a $500 deposit to insure that they'll return. Detailed information packets available upon request.

C "I'm gonna have a pastrami on
white bread with mayonnaise and
tomatoes and lettuce...."

Eating, Nibbling, Noshing,
Chowing Down, Pigging Out

11 LA's Best Bites, from Morning to Night

You've had your first cup of coffee. Now what?

Best Morning Pastries

Some Crust Bakery With a trend towards frozen doughs and packaged mixes, more and more bakeries are opting to cover up with size what they sometimes lack in quality. But not so here, where the proof is in the pastry. Though a second location is scheduled to open on Melrose in summer '89, until then, you won't think twice about driving out to Claremont for their flaky croissants, fruit-filled danishes, or sugar-free (dairy-free) muffins (yes, these ones actually taste like muffins). For a bite of their extraordinary homemade sticky buns—a classic cinnamon-roll dough dripping with caramel and pecans—you'll even go at rush hour. 119 Yale Avenue, Claremont; (714) 621-9772.

Best Donuts

The patrol cars may be lined up two-deep in front of the well-known chains, but in the policeman's line of work, convenience often takes priority to taste. The real food-savvy cops fight to work the Westwood beat, where for 21 years, **Stan's Corner Donut Shoppe** (10948 Weyburn Avenue, Westwood; 208-8660) has provided LA's premiere wake-up call; most notably, their peanut-butter pocket—a raised donut (stuffed with peanut butter, heavily coated with chocolate icing, then topped with chocolate chips) that's so perfect, it doesn't crumble, it melts. . . . This long-standing favorite, however, is facing fresh competition from a stylish newcomer: **Designer Donuts** (6660 Sunset Boulevard, Hollywood; 463-7079), the unofficial donut maker to the stars, whose premium quality rocky road, dutch apple crunch, and blueberries and creme varieties have found a place in the hearts (and stomachs) of the casts of *Cheers, Moonlighting, Family Ties,* and more.

Best Glass of Juice

Beverly Hills Juice Club The Baskin-Robbins of juice bars with over 31 fresh-squeezed choices available. Whether straight up, blended, or whipped into a smoothie, you'll find it delicious to drink to your health. 8382 Beverly Boulevard, LA; 655-8300.

John O'Groats Oatmeal topped with fresh blueberries, French toast flavored with cinnamon and vanilla, eggs perfectly turned, and smoked bacon a half-inch thick. The only problem here is having to order one thing and turn down all the incredible dishes you see on nearby tables. Did I tell you about the home fries seasoned with onions and bell peppers? The baking powder biscuits? The banana pecan pancakes? Ecstasy. This is breakfast as good as breakfast gets, in a homey environment that would make you swear your mom was in the kitchen— assuming, of course, that Mom was an excellent cook. 10516 W. Pico Boulevard, West LA; 204-0692.

Best All-American Breakfast

Caffe Latte This offshoot of Hugo's offers much of the same great food as its West Hollywood counterpart but in a Miracle Mile mini-mall environment that's pleasantly void of its predecessor's show-biz hustle. Maybe the wheeling and dealing is only subdued, but the main reason people are here is to eat. And what's to eat is outstanding: eggs scrambled with prosciutto and hot Italian sausage, orange ginger pancakes, cinnamon raisin French toast, and the praiseworthy Pasta Mama (with parsley, garlic, parmesan, and eggs): an energy-boosting, heaping helping of complex carbohydrates that will leave you wondering why you never had pasta for breakfast before. 6254 Wilshire Boulevard, LA; 936-5213.

Best Not-So-American Breakfast

Cafe Mambo Light pours in the front windows of this small converted house, bounces off the screaming yellow walls, and highlights the whimsical Allee Willis artwork. Welcome to Mambo madness. You may be tucked away in a burgeoning area just steps off lower Melrose, but unexpectedly, the sensational Caribbean-inspired fare defies the trendy turf. It's hard to imagine a better way to start the day than with the fantastic chilaquiles—a scramble of eggs, hot sausage, tortillas, and salsa—though thoughts of huevos negros (poached eggs on toast with a spicy black pepper sauce), shrimp omelettes, passion fruit salad, and moist banana muffins will keep you coming back. Hot food. Cool place. This isn't breakfast, it's a party. 707 Heliotrope, LA; 663-5800.

Mandarin Deli Try to ignore the fact that this is fast becoming a chain; they still offer the best of Chinese breakfast fare, with a quality and taste no one else can match. The cold dishes are wondrous (try the homemade noodles in either sesame or spicy chili peanut sauce), the paper-thin scallion pancakes border on perfection, and the dumplings—steamed, boiled, or fried, bursting with flavor and amazingly greaseless—will have you demanding a branch in your neighborhood. If only they delivered. 701 W. Garvey Avenue, Monterey Park; (818) 570-9795; also at 727 N. Broadway, Chinatown; 356 E. 2nd Street, Downtown; and 9351 Reseda Boulevard, Northridge.

Best Place for Hanging Out All Morning

La Conversacion The quintessential neighborhood patisserie: a tiny storefront, stocked full, with a handful of sidewalk tables made-to-order for lingering over a cup of espresso and the morning paper. Locals swear by the croissants; I've been too busy working on the good-as-they-look jam cookies, macadamia nut hearts, and melanais (tiny hazelnut cakes dotted with fresh raspberries) to notice. Either way, don't leave without checking out the minitarts—fresh fruit atop a perfect crust, the latter lined with a thin coating of rich chocolate. To die for. 2118 Hillhurst Avenue, Los Feliz; 666-9000.

Best Sources for Making Your Own Breakfast

Eggs: **Trafficanda Egg Ranch** The chickens have been moved to Riverside, but their eggs are trekked in daily and sold at this address. And what's wrong with store-bought? Crack open one of these and the delicate fresh taste and bright golden yolk will make the difference obvious. Available by the dozen, but actually, they're cheaper by the flat. 22440 Sherman Way, Canoga Park; (818) 340-1256.

Sausage: **Jody Maroni's Italian Sausage Kingdom** Haute dogs. Orange cumin chicken, curried lamb, maple pork, duck with cilantro and beer . . . with so many excellent choices, you really can't go wrong. But even though they're now for sale at selected Westside markets (Vicente Foods, Santa Glen, and the Beverly Hills Mrs. Gooch's), do yourself a favor and stop and shop at Maroni's boardwalk stand. Here the variety is greater and you'll get to taste and sample as well as get to buy. It's his theory that once you've tried just one, you'll want to have them all. And he's right. 2011 Ocean Front Walk, Venice; 306-1995.

Pancake Mix: **Dupar's Coffee Shop** Forget the grocery store processed stuff. Dupar's pancakes are legendary; better yet, they can also be yours at home. Ask and they're only too pleased to sell you a styrofoam container of premixed batter to go. All you have to do is turn on the griddle, pour, and flip. And lie that you made them from scratch. Third Street at Fairfax, LA; 933-8446; plus four other locations.

You already buy your wines, cheeses, nuts, baked goods, coffee, and frozen foods at **Trader Joe's**. As for the rest . . .

La Brea Circus The stores have all the charm of a combination bomb shelter and holding bin for a garage sale, but like Mom always told me, appearances can be deceiving. The food sections here come packed to the proverbial gills, piled high with gourmet cookies, candies, and condiments as well as specialty items and quality brand name canned and packaged goods, all at savings of 15 to 50 percent. The stock varies, but expect to find at least something you will need: imported pastas and olive oils, crocks of Pommery mustard, giant wheels of brie, dirt-cheap tins of butter cookies, and the best prices in town on Haagen Dazs and Entenmann's. 852 N. La Brea, LA; 466-7231; additional location at 17641 Vanowen, Van Nuys; (818) 345-5650.

The Southland Farmers Market Association A gourmet's flea market of food, usually held once a week in 12 different locations throughout LA. Not only will you have the chance to buy quality produce at great prices, but the range of choices far exceeds what you'll find in most commercial markets. In addition to the fruits and vegetables, there are stands offering fresh fish, flowers, and eggs. Everything sold is produced by the seller or their immediate family. 749-9551.

Special Foods International A restaurant supplier (and not just for any local restaurant, but primarily for all the biggies, like Spago, Valentino, Michael's, Trumps, and Citrus) that at selected hours in the week (usually 10 A.M. to 4 P.M. on Saturdays) is open to the public. This is a premiere source for quality goods, with prices that could actually make eating white truffles and caviar a possibility. Everything is fresh and flown in daily; the selection— from free-range chickens, Louisiana crawfish, and New Zealand John Dory to exotic, out-of-season fruits and white Argentine asparagus—goes beyond outstanding. One trip here and the Irvine Ranch will start to look like K-Mart. 1225 Broadway, Santa Monica; 395-1783.

Diamond Bakery Corn rye or raisin pumpernickel; either one as good as New York's best. 335 N. Fairfax, LA; 655-0534.

Il Fornaio The filone is outstanding: a white-flour Italian bread, best plain or flavored with rosemary. The crust could win awards. 301 N. Beverly Drive, Beverly Hills; 550-8330; plus four additional locations.

Michel Richard Round French loaves, perfectly dark-baked and crunchy, as well as excellent croissants. 310 S. Robertson Boulevard, LA; 275-5707.

La Brea Bakery Finally, a true French baguette in LA. Skinnier, so it's more crust than crumb—and what a crust it is. Incomparable country dinner rolls, too, that are fast becoming a staple at the city's chicest restaurants. 624 S. La Brea Avenue, LA; 939-6813.

Pioneer Boulangerie Try the dense and chewy sourdough in a wonderfully crackly crust. The country-style Basque loaf is a must. 2012 Main Street, Santa Monica; 399-1405.

J&T Bread Bin No one single focus here, just good breads, particularly the Hungarian cinnamon, the cheese-onion, and their popular "monkey bread" (loaves of egg bread, rich in butter, that pull apart for easy eating). Stall 300, Farmers Market, 6333 W. 3rd Street, LA; 936-0785.

Carrillo's Tortilleria Handmade flour and corn tortillas—tender, delicate, and delicious—and still warm from the griddle. Eaten with just a sprinkling of salt, they're addicting. 19744 Sherman Way, Canoga Park; (818) 887-6118.

Best Sunday Brunch

Saddle Peak Lodge A lovely drive through Malibu Canyon leads you to a picturesque rustic hunting lodge with a sweeping outdoor patio. Hollywood couldn't art direct a better brunching place than this (see "Wanted: A Great Spot to Tie the Knot"). And you'd be hard-pressed to find a better midday meal. The basket of rolls, biscuits, cornbread, and mini-muffins disproves the old adage, "Don't fill up on bread"; they're so incredible that you'd be a fool not to. For an appetizer, you could choose a chilled stewed rhubarb or fresh fruit doused in champagne, but you *should* choose the creamy strawberry soup, as rich and luscious as any good dessert. The main courses only get better: poached eggs and crab cakes with caviar; red flannel hash; thick, juicy pork chops (alongside sweet potatoes sauteed with apples and spices); the quintessential ham and eggs. When you're done, just relax over coffee and soak up the peaceful mountain air. If God wasn't resting on Sundays, no doubt He'd be eating here. (Prix fixe: $19.75; reservations are essential.) 419 Cold Canyon Road, Calabasas; (818) 340-6029.

Cafe des Artistes This is one of those undiscovered addresses that you hate to mention for fear you'll never get a table again. Located next to the Stages Theater on a nondescript residential block, and masked by a row of hedges, this charming bungalow-turned-restaurant seems more befitting to Carmel than the heart of Hollywood. Come early to assure yourself a seat on the sun-drenched front patio, where you can sip champagne and listen to a classical trio play. Then turn your attention towards the buffet line: a filling selection of pâtés, breads, fruits, salads, meats, and desserts. At $12.50, this is one of the best all-you-can-eat brunching deals in town. Just try and keep it to yourself, okay? 1534 N. McCadden Place, Hollywood; 461-6889.

Best Little-Known Sunday Brunch

1. Ham on Rye: **The Apple Pan** A perfect combination: paper-thin slices of quality Virginia ham are piled high, the saltiness cut by mustard and counterbalanced by the nutty flavor of Swiss cheese. 10801 W. Pico Boulevard, West LA; 475-3585.

Best Sandwiches . . . eight great ways for eating hand to mouth

2. BLT: **Kokomo Cafe** Simple and straightforward: double-smoked bacon, leafy organic lettuce, and ruby red tomatoes layered between slices of hard-core sourdough. Served with curly Qs, sweet potato chips, or a spicy peanut slaw. Go for the fries. Located in the southwest corner, Farmers Market. 6333 W. Third Street, LA; 933-0773.

3. French Toast Sandwich: **Stroozette** A gourmet twist on a childhood favorite. Peanut butter and bananas smeared between two pieces of very good French toast, with whipped strawberry butter on the side. 4243 Overland Avenue, Culver City; 559-6834.

4. Panino Angeli: **Angeli Caffe** Simplicity at its best. Crisp baked halves of an Italian roll (made, by the way, from their incredible pizza dough) overflow with tomatoes, fresh mozzarella, basil, and olive oil. The panino rustico (marinated chicken breast, raisins, arugula, and mustard) is further proof that there's not a bad food to be had here. 7274 Melrose Avenue, LA; 936-9086; also at Trattoria Angeli, 11651 Santa Monica Boulevard, West LA; 478-1191.

5. Chicken Torta: **El Capricho** Mexico's answer to the submarine. Grilled chicken, cheese, avocado, tomatoes, onions, and peppers are spooned into a tiny torpedo-shaped roll; a sort of burrito on a bun. 317 S. Broadway, Downtown; 617-2269.

6. Pressed Sandwich: **Trumps** A round French loaf is hollowed out, stuffed with chunks of fried chicken, brie, bacon, and onion, then grilled in a croque monsieur–type sandwich press. All very upper crust. 8764 Melrose Avenue, W. Hollywood; 855-1480.

7. Vegetarian: **242 Cafe** Representing all the basic trendy food groups: spinach, grilled eggplant, teleme cheese, roasted red peppers, marinated artichoke hearts, and sun-dried tomatoes, on a chewy French baguette. 242 N. Pacific Coast Highway, Laguna Beach; (714) 494-2444.

8. Chinese Roast Pork: **The Subway** Lean slices of pork on garlic bread, with plum sauce and hot mustard. It tastes as good as it sounds. 4037 Radford, Studio City; (818) 760-9977.

Best Scones

Rose Tree Cottage The Daughters of Darjeeling have staked their reputation on this one and they'll get no argument from me. The scones here are gems, with a wonderful biscuity quality and just the right amount of currants. Enjoy them, with Devonshire cream and fresh strawberry preserves, in the picture-perfect tea room, or pick up a dozen to go. On second thought, you better make that two. 824 E. California Boulevard, Pasadena; (818) 793-3337.

Best Late Lunch

City Restaurant Forget worrying about where you can go to get something to eat after midnight; the real problem is scoring a decent lunch after 2:30 in the afternoon. While high teas are fine, they're heavy on the sugar, and servings hardly make a mouthful. But thankfully, City offers a special late lunch menu, daily from 3 to 5 P.M. And though it changes constantly, what a menu it is: tuna tartare, roasted red peppers with feta cheese, Thai melon salad, rare roast beef and horseradish on onion naan, and the best gnocchi in town. Top it all off with a superlative cup of coffee and one of their excellent desserts. 180 S. La Brea Avenue, LA; 938-2155.

Best Happy Hour

Grand Avenue Bar A class act, in deep brown tones, with Japanese tiles, marble tables, and good art on the walls. Vintage wine is poured by the glass, they don't bruise the gin, and the complimentary hors d'oeuvres are a mix of upscale Mexican and Chinese. But the real attraction here is live music, every Monday through Friday from 5 to 9 P.M., with a different style of jazz—from blues to salsa—offered nightly. Biltmore Hotel, 506 S. Grand Avenue, Downtown; 624-1011.

The Beverly Restaurant and Market Large plump birds are roasted crisp and juicy, that ideal combination of texture and taste. While the chili-rubbed, Jamaican jerk, and lemon tarragon varieties are all superb, the garlic rosemary, moist and bursting with flavor, will leave you speechless. Which is fine, since you won't have to worry about offending anyone with your breath. 342 N. Beverly Drive, Beverly Hills; 274-4271.

Best Take-Out Chicken

Caioti It wasn't even six years ago that LA finally wised up, stopped trying to imitate the perfect N.Y. pizza, and invented a version of its own. Caioti owner Ed Ladou was the first pizza chef at Spago (and later, the consultant to the California Pizza Kitchens) and while his recipes and techniques have been cloned, chained, and copied, he has obviously kept some small secret to himself. Not too surprising, the pies here are superior, ranging from the traditional (pepperoni mushroom) to the trendy (roast garlic and glazed shallots with smoked gouda; barbecue chicken) to the chance to design your own. But what ends up on top really doesn't matter, because here the crust's the thing—slightly smoky, crisp yet chewy, and ideal for snacking without any adornment at all. 2100 Laurel Canyon Boulevard, LA; 650-2988; or 8280 Sunset Boulevard, W. Hollywood; 656-2093.

Best Pizza

Atlantic Avenue Area, Monterey Park Stretching down Atlantic Avenue, between the San Bernadino and Pomona freeways, this new Chinatown boasts hundreds of quality restaurants. Chief among them: **Wonder Seafood** (try the giant scallops or baked crabs with garlic), **Dragon Regency** (for their snake soup and crispy Double Pleasure Sole), **Fragrant Vegetable** (vegetarian, but still terrific), and **Harbor Village** (rumored to have the best dim sum in town). But names don't really matter; wander about, then wander in at will. It's practically impossible to find a bad meal in the lot.

Best Chinese Food

Authentic Cafe It would be easy to miss this tiny place—just seven tables plus seven stools at a counter—if it weren't for the crowd outside. And it would be easy to dismiss it, thanks to taqueria-trendy whitewashed walls and baby cactus all around. But hold on. While you will find a smattering of Santa Fe–style dishes on the menu

Best Place to Eat When Everyone Wants Something Different

(very good fresh corn tamales and Yucatan chicken, for starters), owner/chef Roger Hayot has much more up his sieve. Want Italian? His pizzas and pastas are terrific. Chinese? The fiery Szechuan dumplings will transport you to Beijing. Down-home cooking? There's stick-to-your-ribs meat loaf, chicken pot pie in a cornbread crust, and all-American desserts worth blowing the diet for. The Authentic thumbs its nose at a cardinal restaurant rule ("Too many specialties and nothing is special"), not only serving up something for everyone, but doing it delectably well. Build a better mousetrap and the world beats a path to your door. 7605 Beverly Boulevard, LA; 939-4626.

Best Place to Eat with People Who Can Never Make Up Their Minds

Killer Shrimp No worry about them hemming and hawing here. This streamlined mini-mall restaurant makes deciding what to have a breeze, inasmuch as there's just one thing on the menu. But there'll be no complaints. Fresh Louisiana shrimp are flown in daily, then cooked to order in a simmering spicy sauce of beer, butter, garlic, herbs, and spices. Chunks of crusty French bread, served on the side, make dunking a new experience. The name is brilliant. So is the food. 523 Washington Street, Marina del Rey; 578-2293.

Best Restaurants with Entertainment

Verdi That rare place where the food and music are on equal par, and both are par excellence. Glorious Italian fare (prix fixe: $28.50) is served between quality performances from opera, operettas, and Broadway musicals, courtesy of a resident company of 22 young professionals. But what *is* is only surpassed by what isn't, and there isn't a cover charge, a drink minimum, or a bad seat to be had. In fact, so committed are the owners to wanting all music lovers to enjoy their restaurant, that special "light supper" and "just dessert" menus (from $9 for pastry, cognac, and coffee to $13.25 for pasta, salad, and a glass of wine) are available nightly at the bar. 1519 Wilshire Boulevard, Santa Monica; 393-0706.

Bubbles Balboa Club A red-carpeted walkway leads you underneath a neon-lit marquee, past a curve of glass bricks, and through a set of stainless steel doors with porthole windows. Entering Bubbles, a stylish moderne supper club and restaurant, is like stepping into a scene from a Busby Berkeley musical, one where leggy cigarette girls hawk their wares, giant champagne glasses adorn the walls, and a spectacular floor-to-ceiling clear glass tube blows out a constant stream of bubbles. Dine on '30s favorites, but with an '80s flavor: lamb chops, duck, or grilled fish and sirloin, in a sea of mint cream, raspberry, or pecan butter sauces. Then head to the bar for the best in swing and jazz bands (The Ink Spots are featured regularly), and relive the days when Newport Beach was a sultry summer resort. 111 Palm Street, Newport Beach; (714) 675-9093.

Duplex A mom-and-pop place, with a very hip mom and pop. Mark Carter and Stephanie Chiacos have created the kind of restaurant where it's more like going home than going out to dinner. The bar is cozy and the rose-colored upper dining area inviting, but it is the front room, with its high ceilings, skylights, wall of glass windows, and mix-and-match chairs that urges you to have a seat and stay. As does the food, a serious but uncomplicated mix of tea-smoked chicken on a spicy noodle pancake, eggplant-and-goat-cheese napoleon, salmon in avocado sauce, or filet with 11 ingredients. The cappuccino is first-rate, as it should be to keep up with the excellent desserts (Carter was once the noted pastry chef at Bernard's in the Biltmore Hotel). The whimsical map-covered menus are marked to point out, "You are here." No doubt you'll be glad that you are. 1930 Hillhurst Avenue, Los Feliz; 663-2430.

Best Neighborhood Restaurants

Five Feet The sign out front actually reads: 5'0". What's in a name? God only knows. But here is contemporary Chinese food, served with forks instead of chopsticks, in a smart room of exposed bricks and beams and quirky cartoon murals. Though still in his twenties, owner Michael Kang was an architect before he was a chef, and his plates (and place) reflect it: whole deep-fried catfish in a spicy citrus sauce, blackened sushi, hot braised prawns, mussels in black bean ginger, goat cheese won ton, and crispy egg rolls made with corn tortillas, each styled in a manner worthy of a 9.9 for artistic expression. Don't let the Orange County address put you off. For the same time you spend waiting at the popular LA eateries (yes, even when you have a reservation) you could already be seated, happily eating here. Five Feet by any other name would still be a giant. 328 Glenneyre, Laguna Beach; (714) 497-4955.

Shiro A simple room provides the perfect understated backdrop for some amazingly good food. Chef Hideo Yamashiro combines ultrafresh fish with a flare for French flavors. His appetizers are stunning, particularly the ravioli, made with won ton wrappers, then stuffed with shrimp and salmon mousse and served alongside a basil or fennel sauce, depending on the night. The tuna sashimi comes between slices of avocado and topped with limes, and the seafood salad is simply magnificent, piled high with mussels, clams, shrimp, scallops, and squid in a subtle herb dressing. This is clear-tasting food, with a light, healthy touch; you will definitely have room for dessert. (Definitely try the exquisite creme brulee.) My only complaint with Shiro is that it isn't in my neighborhood. 1505 Mission Street, S. Pasadena; (818) 799-4774.

Magdalena's A great secret address. Hidden amongst car dealers, pawn shops, and industrial buildings, this pleasant two-room cafe offers a menu similar to many upscale restaurants . . . until you take a look at the prices. Dinners—featuring fresh wild game, Norwegian salmon, and an outstanding duck in blackberry sauce—run a reasonable $13 to $25, and that includes soup, salad, a basket of cheese straws, artful vegetables, and a handsome plate of truffles, merringues, palmiers, and tuiles. Sophisticated food in an unlikely setting. 17818 Bellflower Boulevard, Bellflower; 925-6551.

Best Restaurant on the Way to the Airport

Versailles This place is no palace, but it does serve up the cheapest, choicest Cuban chow in town. Ideally located just five minutes in either direction from southbound La Cienega or the southbound 405, it has recently expanded, making it now feasible to get you in and get you out in time to get your plane. No hurry? Still no need to bother with a menu. There is no choice here but to order the roasted chicken, one of the best you'll ever eat: a monstrous crisp-skinned wonder, dripping in a citrus vinegar marinade, topped with slices of sweet onions and stuffed with enough garlic to halt a host of vampires. Forget what Mother told you and don't brush before you board your flight. It'll better your chances of winding up with three seats to yourself. 10319 Venice Boulevard, Culver City; 558-3168.

Best Desserts in a Restaurant

City Restaurant One of these days I'm going to walk into City, forget all about the parsnip chips and tandoori chicken, order six desserts, and call it a night. Which six will be the problem. The double-decker bakery case is an eyeful, teasing you with mocha almond tart, lemon hazelnut meringue, walnut caramel torte, red yam flan, apple spice cake (topped with hot cream cheese), and chocolate souffle in an espresso sauce. And that's just on the bottom shelf. There are fresh fruit pies and tarts, four different chocolate cakes, creme caramel, bread pudding, date nut bars, chunky saucer-sized cookies, and a silly Hostess-like cupcake that duplicates the real thing with top-of-the-line tastes. Sweet dreams are made of these. 180 S. La Brea Avenue, LA; 938-2155.

Best Bedtime Treats

Best Chocolate Chip Cookie: **Fred Segal Cafe & Eats** Only a dozen dozen are made daily. No nuts, no gourmet gimmicks . . . just semisweet chocolate chips in a classic toll house dough. The results are taste-bud perfect: slightly crisp around the edges, then soft and chewy all the way through. Sorry, Mrs. Fields. 8112 Melrose Avenue, LA; 653-6918; also at 500 Broadway, Santa Monica; 394-0199.

Best Ice Cream: **Robin Rose** There's a new line of sorbets, quality hand-dipped chocolates, and caramel and hot fudge sauces worth writing home about. You'll also find liqueur-flavored "Truffle Cups," specialty cookies (try the triple fudge), and elaborate custom cakes. But wondrous as they all are, it's still the ice cream you should scream for. The apple a la mode (slices of apples, brandy-soaked raisins, bits of English toffee, cinnamon, and walnuts) is tempting; the devil's food cookies and cream (the cookies are baked on the premises) are hard to resist; and the California pistachio (whole roasted nuts in a white chocolate base) will drive you crazy. But for a pint of their raspberry chocolate truffle (bittersweet chocolate ice cream, a puree of black raspberries, and chunks of chocolate Chambord truffles), you'd probably sell your mother. 215 Rose Avenue, Venice; 399-1774; additional locations in Beverly Hills, Pasadena, West LA, and Woodland Hills.

Best Pie: **The Apple Pan** Despite the name, the best choices—either by the slice at the U-shaped counter or whole and packed to go—are the banana (with more bananas than custard) and the boysenberry (luscious whole fresh fruit, but sans the overwhelming glaze), each topped with a heady layer of fresh whipped cream and in a crust the French would envy. (The best apple pie, for the record, is the slightly sweet, slightly tart, double-crusted wonder found at **Fred Segal Cafe & Eats**.) 10801 W. Pico Boulevard, West LA; 475-3585.

Best Tips for Dieters Who Are Constantly Hungry

Frozen Yogurt: **Glacier Bay** What distinguishes this LA branch of a Florida-based chain from the plethora of frozen yogurt stores popping up on corners everywhere, is that they carry not one, but six different brands of frozen soft serve—Honeyhill, Gisé, American Glacé, Bonjour, Colombo, and Vitari—and in a variety of changing flavors. Try the Orange Vitari (made from 99-percent fruit and fruit juice, with no dairy, no fat, no cholesterol, and no added sugar), twenty calories per ounce and so good that the ice cream industry should declare it a Communist plot. 8253 Santa Monica Boulevard, W. Hollywood; 654-4332.

Lo-Cal Ranch Dressing: **Caplan's Deli** A nutritionist tipped me off to this one. What's in it is a mystery; how it tastes is not. Thick, creamy, and (whether mixed with tuna, smeared on sandwiches, or ladled over baked potatoes) too good to be good for you. 18635 Devonshire, Northridge; (818) 368-5707.

Mentioned Elsewhere

Spago, Millie's, Chin Chin See "Best Bets for Tourists, Helpful Hints for Hosts."

The Ivy, "Best Margaritas," Geoffrey's See "LA Laws."

Fountain Coffee Room (Beverly Hills Hotel), World's Oldest McDonald's, Donut Hole, Tail o' the Pup, The Source See "LA Landmarks."

Seafood Bay, Rex il Restorante, Yee Mee Loo, Gorky's Cafe, Gasoline Alley See "The Best Cheap Dates in LA."

Gondola Getaways, Ultimate Dimensions in Dining See "The Best Ways and Means to Celebrate a Special Occasion."

Wheeler Hot Springs See "The Best Ways to Spend a Sunny Sunday in LA."

West Valley Occupational Center Bake Shop See "LA's Best Undiscovered Discount Stores."

Trattoria Angeli, Bodacious Buns, Mrs. Beasley's Unforgettable Chocolate Chip Cookies, Gertie's Cheesecakes, Perfect Picnics, Stanford Gift Baskets See "Say It with Food."

Specific Pacific, A La Carte See "House Callers."

Cafe Beignet See "Ten Unusual Places to Throw a Party."

The Venice Patisserie, Seafood Emporium, Noonan's/The Pit, In and Out Burgers See "There's No Place Like Home."

Chez Helene, Marix Tex Mex Playa, Women's Assistance League Tea Room, Rebecca's, Camelions, Prego, Trumps See "Private Rooms for Private Parties."

Saddle Peak Lodge See "Wanted: A Great Spot to Tie the Knot."

D

"Whoever said money can't buy happiness didn't know where to shop."

Stores, Sales, Services, and Assorted Sundries

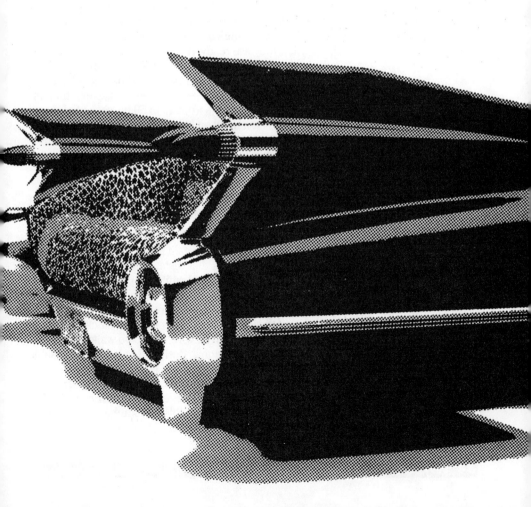

12

LA's Best Undiscovered Discount Stores

Because buying retail is stupid

Class for the Mass

Home Express Step through the front doorway (which resembles a new-wave Mayan temple), circumvent the granite check-out counters, grab a black-and-turquoise laminated cart, and go. Welcome to the discount store for the '90s, a slick, sleek, hi-tech warehouse (part Esprit, part Crate & Barrel, and a little bit Toys R Us) with value prices on housewares, textiles, electronics, ready-to-assemble furniture, and everything conceivable for organizing your home. Peppered in with the typical bargain fare are names like Alessi, Sasaki, Techline, Metrokane, and Hall. Scattered throughout the stock are trendy items normally reserved for Melrose Avenue–type shops: neon phones, glazed terra-cotta dinnerware, zolatone-finished headboards,and multicolored aluminum tea kettles that hum when they are ready. A central area houses up-to-the-minute themed merchandise (geared, for example, to Christmas, back-to-school or beach and barbecue) that changes according to the season. (Yes, yes, everything is discounted, with savings from 15 to 50 percent.) Salespeople are even helpful and abundant. And best of all, they offer a money-back guarantee if you are able to find any of their merchandise at a lower price anywhere else. God as my witness, you'll never have to shop Adray's again. Three locations: Edinger & Gothard, Huntington Beach; (714) 892-2592. 8341 La Palm Avenue, Buena Park; (714) 739-4663. Del Amo Fashion Center, Torrance; 371-4663.

Kitchen Help

Avery Services Any bargain hunter worth their pinched pennies knows that restaurant supply stores can be a savings gold mine. And while shopping at most is akin to going into battle, Avery is a pleasant surprise: neat, organized, and 90,000 square feet of just about everything that goes into a kitchen. From stockpots to stainless steel bowls, from wire whisks to walk-in coolers, all of it is simple, functional, designed to last, and available in a variety of sizes. Need a novel gift for the entire family? Consider a hot fudge dispenser, soft-pretzel warmer, or movie theater popcorn machine. Strapped for space? Let a coffee-shop corner booth double as a kitchen table. Avery has all of this, plus Calphalon pots, Silverstone pans, Wolf ranges, and Waring bar blenders (half the price of what you'll pay for similar-looking, less sturdy commercial models). You can even buy your favorite chefs their own set of whites. 905 E. Second Street, Downtown; 624-7832.

The Dish Factory Get downtown and get dirty. Unlike Avery, this place looks like the restaurant supply store that it is. Everything is buried under dust, but before you turn up your nose and walk away, dig in, sift through, and uncover what has to be the most incredible assortment of heavy-duty dinnerware in town. We're talking vintage '50s and '50s-style diner china here, from manufacturers like Buffalo, H.F. Coors, and Homer Laughlin—some of it plain, some of it patterned, and some even bearing the names of restaurants, country clubs, and private women's colleges. There are stacks and stacks, rows and rows of plates, bowls, cups, saucers, creamers, mugs, ramekins, butter dishes, and ceramic water pitchers—tons of hip stuff. Prices are unbelievably low; buy by the dozen and it's tantamount to stealing. 310 S. Los Angeles Street, Downtown; 687-9500.

Almost (and) Perfect English China You might not expect to find a great discount source on this yup-and-coming stretch of Ventura Boulevard, but this crowded little shop spotlights Villeroy and Boch, Spode, Royal Doulton, Portmeirion, Wedgwood, and most brands of fine English bone china in open stock and at 25 percent below retail. Jolly good, yes, but not as good as the potential savings you'll find on the barely flawed china (in most of the same makes and patterns) that they also sell here. These are pieces that have been rejected because of minor color variations or slight painting errors; none of them are chipped. What they are is indistinguishable from the real thing. Lots of teacups and teapots, too. 14519 Ventura Boulevard, Sherman Oaks; (818) 905-6650.

Great tabletop buys are equally abundant at two discount outlets connected to major LA manufacturers. **The Mikasa Factory Store** (20642 S. Fordyce, Carson; 537-9344) features first-quality china, stemware, flatware, and gifts, at 45 to 75 percent off list. They carry much of the regular line (missing are a number of patterns available exclusively to certain retailers), as well as close-outs, discontinueds, and (here's one way to keep ahead of the Joneses) test patterns of what could be some of next year's new designs. Sub-lines produced by Mikasa are available as well: names like Studio Nova, Mikasa Kids,

High Road to China

Oscar de la Renta, and Daniel Hechter (yes, he does dishes). Call first to make sure they have what you want in stock, and at the price you want it.

You may not know the name, but you're bound to recognize the plate. **Metlox/Poppytrail Pottery** (407 Manhattan Beach Boulevard, Manhattan Beach; 545-1977) has been around since 1927 and theirs is quintessential California ware—bright, stylish, colorful, and fun. "Colorstax" is an '80s update of classic '40s dishes, in a rainbow of cool hues; the oversized 16-ounce cups and saucers designed to match (and perfect for cafe au lait or double cappuccino) are a must-have on their own. So are the fish-shaped casseroles, the black-and-white holstein-patterned serving pieces, and the "California Harvest" cannisters (done to look like local fruits and veggies). Metlox makes the kind of stuff that makes you smile, especially here, when you can get it all at wholesale.

Save Face

Max Factor Cosmetic Outlet Located in the landmark tower building (now beauty museum) that was once home to their corporate office, this store promises big name-brand cosmetics and designer fragrances at discounts up to 70 percent. Most of it, obviously, is from Max Factor, but sister companies such as Halston, Almay, and Mary Quant are often stocked as well. Before leaving, check around for leftovers from special premium offers (such as oversized sweatshirts or overnight bags); these are often the best deals in the place—except for the fact that, in the heart of Hollywood, there's plenty of free parking on the side. 1666 N. Highland Avenue, Hollywood; 463-6164.

Similarly, a trip to **Freeport International** (1058 S. Main Street, Downtown; 745-7823) will leave you smelling like a rose. This wholesale distributor offers top names in top scents (names like Nina Ricci, Chloe, Opium, Picasso, and Paco the last time I was there) at top savings (often less than 50 percent, even cheaper by the dozen). No rip-offs formulated to smell like something else; here it's the genuine thing.

Consigning Women

The Address Maureen Clavin's stylish store is the current Queen of Resale, offering chic castoffs and designer duds from some very well-known closets. She's not saying who, but she will say what—quality gowns, suits, leathers, suedes, and accessories, bearing labels like Adolpho, Chanel, Armani, and Valentino. All barely worn (some have probably never been worn at all) and all at a fraction of their original cost. While the rest of the merchandise available here is new (bought directly from manufacturers, so you save on it as well), I challenge you, without studying tags, to figure out which is which. In fact, the resale items are possibly the better, culled from an exclusive list of rich and famous ladies who (lucky for bargain hunters) risk social shame when seen in the same thing twice. Just pray that none of them show up at the same ceremony, party, or benefit as you. They might recognize their clothes. 1116 Wilshire Boulevard, Santa Monica; 394-1406.

A slew of other stores also proves that penny-wise doesn't necessarily mean fashion-foolish. At the top of anyone's list should be **The Place and Company** (8820 S. Sepulveda Boulevard, LA; 645-1539), which, for 25 years, has kept customers coming back for first-rate resale casual and evening wear, and which counts Joan Collins among its sources (the proceeds from her goods go to charity). **Chic Conspiracy**, with two locations (350 S. La Cienega Boulevard, LA; 657-1177; and 10955 W. Pico Boulevard, West LA; 475-5542), receives shipments from all over the world, enabling them to supply the normal and more, including some men's clothes (La Cienega store only) and hard-to- find larger women's sizes.

For Kids Only If the atmosphere and prices in this merchandise-packed store are typically budget basement, the trendy togs that fill the racks are anything but. Hand-knit sweaters, bomber jackets, jazzy jumpsuits, European cottons, pleated pants, leather shoes . . . all the prerequisites to make your kids the darlings of the playground set. Whether it's for boys, girls,or babies, whether it's domestic or imported, what you'll find here is stylish, well-designed, and guaranteed to turn their fashion-conscious little heads. The discounts of 30 to 60 percent should help keep you from losing yours. 746 N. Fairfax Avenue, LA; 650-4885.

Dress for Recess

Knowing that most parents hate to pay premium prices because most kids grow out of stuff faster than it goes out of style, other children's shops have jumped on the bargain bandwagon. Not to be missed: **Samplings** (10117 W. Washington Boulevard, Culver City; 204-1085), which combines California's newest designers with what could be the largest selection of Oshkosh in town, and **Pee Wee** (10590 W. Pico Boulevard, West LA; 204-1463), where the bold-colored overalls (made from Hawaiian shirt-type fabrics) and high-fashion denims are among the things sure to assure your kid the best seat in the sandbox. . . . More routine, but equally worth your while, is the **Carter's Factory Outlet** (864 Wagonwheel Road, Oxnard; 805-485-3500), a veritable grandmother's gold mine with its incredible savings on the basic layette (and anything else Carter's up to size 14). Smart shoppers with an eye for fashion will discover that this is also the place to find discounted Baby Dior, since Carter's (get this) manufactures Dior's entire infant line.

It Suits Your Case

H. Savinar Luggage Get ready to pack your bags. With the money you'll save buying them here, you can easily afford a vacation. Most major brands are represented: Hartman, Lark, Ventura, Andiamo, and Tumi. There is a slew of purses and business portfolios as well, and great prices on such "power tools" as Halliburton briefcases (both silver and gold) and Day Runner Organizers. And even if what you want isn't stocked, as long as it's produced domestically, they will happily (and readily) order it for you. Two locations: 4625 W. Washington Boulevard, LA; 938-2501. 6931 Topanga Canyon Boulevard, Canoga Park; (818) 703-1313.

Painless Recovery

Diamond Foam and Fabric Top-quality upholstery fabrics of the same ilk (and silk) as those in the Pacific Design Center showrooms, but with prices so low I've seen decorators shopping here. So much for trade secrets. Diamond's stock is an amassment of sample bolts, test patterns, last year's lines, special orders, color variations, and whatever else looks good. Give owner Jason Ashe an inkling of what you want, and seconds later he is pulling down, rolling out, and throwing around an endless assortment of great things—not to mention more one liners than Henny Youngman. You probably won't love it all, but you will love that there isn't a calico print or polished cotton in the bunch. Take your chairs . . . please. 611 S. La Brea Avenue, LA; 931-8148.

Student Body Work

West Valley Occupational Center While obviously not a discount store, this trade tech school offers several programs which in turn offer several discount deals. Leading the list: the Auto Repair Workshop. Since the theory here is students learn by doing, the students in the course are always in need of cars to practice on. Which means in return for the basic costs of parts and materials, you can arrange for class members to take care of anything and everything that ails your set of wheels: from mechanical problems, wiring, and body work to paint jobs and upholstery. There's no labor charge, and no worry that you'll get stuck with an expensive transmission when all you really need is a hose. Likewise, trainees in the chef's program offer major savings on the fruits (and fruit-filled goods) of their labors. For only pennies, you can stock up on home-made breads, pies, cakes, and cookies at the Student Bake Shop. Call first, because what's on hand, will depend on what was taught that day. Services are available only when school is in session (from September to June). 6200 Winnetka Avenue, Woodland Hills; (818) 346-3540.

On Beyond Wholesale

Andy Warhol's cookie jars notwithstanding, auctions offer an unexpected excess of undiscovered deals. Particularly police auctions, where on selected Saturdays throughout the year, recovered stolen merchandise that has gone unclaimed goes up for public purchase. While various departments throughout the city schedule similar-type sales, the **LAPD Auction** (always the first Saturdays in April, August, and December; 485-3196) is probably the biggest. Not to mention the ideal spot to find a bicycle or car stereo, as those are the two items most frequently ripped off.

Down in Pico Rivera, the **Public Administrator/ Public Guardian Auction** (write 320 W. Temple, Room 1500, LA 90012) specializes in all kinds of estate sales (be there no will, a contested will, or just the will to sell), holding them two to three times monthly. Though potentially a bargain-hunting heaven, be warned that the quality can vary greatly; still collections, collectibles, and hi-end name items can be found among the junk.

Though not an auction (and though sometimes hit-and-miss), the much-advertised monthly **California Mart Saturday Sale** (exact location can vary; 623-5876) does present a wealth of possibilities: 175 (women's, men's, and children's) clothing manufacturing reps showcasing close to 300 lines and selling it all (primarily left over stock) at well below wholesale. Which is all well and good, but savvy shoppers know that the best buys at the Mart (110 E. Ninth Street, Downtown) are actually found on the last *Friday* of each month. It is then when the more than 1500 showrooms get rid of all their samples (yes, at cost) and quietly, discreetly allow the public in to buy. Most of what you'll find is so new that it has yet to hit the stores. Sizes are limited (mainly six to eight for women, 'medium' for men), but what a great source for extra Christmas gifts.

Discount Hotels/Rental Cars See "Best Bets for Tourists, Helpful Hints for Hosts."

Discount Flowers See "24-Hour LA" and "Best Bets for Parties."

Discount Airline Tickets See "Get Away Without Going Away."

Discount Food See "LA's Best Bites, from Morning to Night."

Discount At-Home Entertaining See "There's No Place Like Home."

Rented Rich

13

*When you don't want to
spend the money and/or can't
afford to buy*

The new furniture looks great, but, c'mon, those framed
O'Keeffe posters on the wall? No problem. Replace them
with the real stuff. **The DeVorzan Gallery** (8687
Melrose Avenue, W. Hollywood; 659-0555) will rent you
anything in their inventory, from Chagall to Picasso to
Miro. They also handle a handful of on-the-rise contemporary artists plus a range of sculptural pieces, including
Auto Art's too-cool-for words, ocelot-covered couch made
from the rear end and back seat of a'59 Caddy. Nothing
here comes cheap—weekly rental fees average ten percent of the gallery's asking price.

Rent a Picasso

A better deal might be to check out the **Rental Gallery**
at the LA County Museum of Art (5905 Wilshire
Boulevard, LA; 857-6500). You will have to be a member
and there is a two-month minimum for rental, but exhibi-
tions (featuring local, emerging artists) change every five
weeks (resulting in an impressively diverse choice of
work), and 75 percent of what you pay is applicable
towards purchase. Days and hours vary, so call ahead.

You can rent cute, you can rent classic, you can even rent
a wreck, but if you really want to keep up with the
Spellings, then the best place to rent is from **Budget's
Exotic Car Collection** (9815 Wilshire Boulevard,
Beverly Hills; 274-9173; or 4500 Lincoln Boulevard,
Marina Del Rey; 821-8200). Rolls, Jaguars, Ferraris,
Bentleys, Range Rovers, Corvette convertibles . . . you
name it, they've got it. Just decide what fits best with how
you want to be perceived (or who it is you need to
impress), and they'll let you borrow the keys. Prices
range from $89 to $400 a day, with 50 free miles.

Rent a Rolls

Be above it all in either a JetRanger big enough for four or
a smaller Hughes 300, courtesy of **Jetcopters** (Van
Nuys Airport; 818-902-0800). For $170 to $420 an hour,
you can make a spectacular entrance, a quick exit, or just
see LA like you've never seen it before.

**Rent a
Helicopter**

Rent a Computer

Organize your life or just test disk-drive before you buy. **Ganton Temporary Computer** (818-901-9978) offers everything you would want or need, from laptops to 386s (from IBM to Apple), and will deliver anywhere (free of charge) from Bakersfield to San Diego. Twenty different printers are also available, running the dot-matrix-to-laser gamut. And while there are no restrictions regarding length of rental time, should you only need the hardware for a day, for a much-lower (in fact, minimal) fee, you are invited to come in and use everything right there.

Rent a Writer

In a city where everybody and their mother is working on a screenplay, **Elayne Lansburg** (818-985-3250) is just plain working, providing a wide range of short-term writing services. Her resume actually includes resumes, in addition to classifieds, personals, speeches, advertising copy . . . even thank-you notes (okay, so money *does* buy everything). But her true forte is writing letters, and in particular, consumer and customer complaints. For around $20 (assuming consultation is minimal), she will figure out who to write, where to reach them, and just what needs to be said. All you'll have to do is sign on the dotted line.

Rent a Designer Gown

At last. Women who need something special for a black-tie event can do what men do and simply rent what they need for the night. **Jeran Design** (8411 Melrose Place, LA; 651-2546) makes one-of-a-kind, hand-beaded, and sequined evening wear, and does so for the likes of Joan Collins, Stephanie Powers, Kim Novak, and Tina Turner. Their couture line retails (at stores like Neiman-Marcus) for $5,000 to $12,000 a pop, but (probably because they started as a costume rental company and still subscribe to fantasy) they regularly stock a small selection of similar-type gowns that they rent on a nightly basis. For an affordable $175, their glitz and glamour can be yours. . . . Similar one-night stands can also be arranged through **Dressed to Kill** (8762 Holloway Drive, W. Hollywood; 652-4334), LA's latest (and largest) lender of ladies' fashions. No hand-me-downs here; these are new clothes, updated each season. You'll find a wide range of styles (from dressy short to elegant long) in a wide range of prices (as low as $50, as high as $400) from an even wider range of designers (figure Bob Mackie, Adolpho, Nina Ricci, and Kevin Hall, to name a few). Better yet, you'll be treated the same as if you were buying instead of just borrowing, inasmuch as any dress will be altered to fit. Accessories run extra, but count on the owners to stock the bag, hat, necklace, bracelet, pin, earrings, and/or gloves you might need to go with it. So go for it. Cher would want you to.

Auntie Mame (1102 S. La Cienega Boulevard, LA; 651-4650) is a vintage clothing store, with the emphasis on furs. This family-owned business buys, sells, cleans, repairs, remodels, and of course, rents them. Their stock is constantly changing, but the real finds here are the classic raccoon coats, in both men's and women's sizes. A one-day rental (great for the USC–UCLA football game) will run you $50 to $100; for a winter trip back east, weekly rates can be arranged.

Rent a Fur

Why limit the premiere of your latest homemade efforts to the confines of your living room TV? Roll out the red carpet and go Hollywood. Unlike other facilities (most of which specialize in film), **Market Street Screening Room** (73 Market Street, Venice; 396-5937) has the setup to handle both half-inch (either VHS or Beta) and three-quarter-inch video. The stylish screening room ($55 to $75 an hour) comes complete with a lobby bar, a ten-foot screen, an eclectic mix of deco theater seats, and room enough for 60. Impress your friends, wow your family, and leave Speilberg shaking in his boots.

Rent a Screening Room

Dreamboats See "LA Laws."

Barton's Horse-Drawn Carriages See "The Best Ways and Means to Celebrate a Special Occasion."

Jukeboxes for Rent, Rent a Trash Bin, and Roschu Prop House See "Best Bets for Parties."

Rent-a-Pony See "Minor Affairs."

Mentioned Elsewhere

14

LA's Most Specialized Specialty Stores

The Last Wound-Up So what if the original is in New York? The sensibilities are far better suited to LA. A mecca for windup toys, in quantities big enough to make Pee Wee Herman green with envy. 7374 Melrose Avenue, LA; 653-6703.

Kaleido See the world through rose-colored glass. Nothing but kaleidoscopes, all shapes and sizes, from $3 to $3600. Kaleidoscopes with real gems, kaleidoscopes you can wear, kaleidoscopes in miniature. . . even a kaleidoscope castle. 8840 Beverly Boulevard (Antiquarius Bldg.), LA; 276-6844.

Footsie One place you won't mind letting them sock it to you. A stupendous stash of everything the well-dressed feet are wearing: solids, stripes, patterns, paisleys, polka dots, and prints—all makes, all fabrics, all sizes. And not for women only; they're stocked knee-high in great things for men and kids as well. So let the other little piggies go to market. Yours should be heading here. 910 Montana Avenue, Santa Monica; 393-7037.

Maps to Anywhere You might get lost finding this place (it occupies two rooms on the second floor of a dingy commercial building) but you'll never get lost once you've been here. A veritable traveler's treasure trove: 10,000 maps, 3,000 book titles (120 on hiking alone), tapes in 60 different languages . . . not to mention globes, videos, dictionaries, phrase books and whatever else it takes to tell you where to go. Due to limited space, only a fraction of the stock is on display, so give a yell if you fail to see what you want. 1514 N. Hillhurst Avenue, Hollywood; 660-2101.

House of Canes Canes made of everything from aluminum to silver. Canes with decorative heads. Canes that conceal swords. Canes that double as fishing poles. Canes with watches or perfume bottles hidden in the handles. Canes complete with hollow shafts that house vial-shaped brandy glasses. Great custom-designed walking sticks, too. Charlie Chaplin would have had a field day here. 5628 Vineland Avenue, N. Hollywood; (818) 769-4007.

Fry's Left Handers A supply store for southpaws. Playing cards with the numbers in all four corners, spatulas and golf clubs with reverse slants, rulers that read from right to left, corkscrews that turn counterclockwise, smear-proof writing pads and notebooks . . . over 150 everyday objects designed to keep you from feeling left out in left field. Ports o' Call, San Pedro; 832-8993.

Vidiots A video holy land—three thousand titles (and going strong) and still not a *Rocky* or *Rambo* in stock. Expect to find anything that's hard to find, including independent and foreign films, cult classics, performance art pieces, experimental projects, and most PBS and BBC documentaries. 302 Pico Boulevard, Santa Monica; 392-8508.

Teddy Bear Country Better than the average bear boutique. Collector caliber, in fact, thanks to an assortment of one-of-a-kind, artist-designed plush with a sprinkling of antique teddys on the side. 23564 Calabasas Road, Calabasas; (818) 702-0848.

Montana Paws Tiny pawprints on the sidewalk give a good inclination of what's in store. An eclectic catalog of cat-shaped and cat-adorned clothing, ceramics, furniture, accessories, and jewelry. Enough to make any cataholic positively catatonic. 1025 Montana Avenue, Santa Monica; 458-7933.

Udderly Perfect No bull here. The hot 'n trendy Holstein has a store all her own, offering an amusing stockyard of black-and-white-patterned products. Everything from pottery and hand-painted clothes to toothbrushes and toilet paper dispensers. The kitchen stools, complete with udders dangling from underneath the seats, are choice. 1201 Highland Avenue, Manhattan Beach; 546-5322; or 740 16th Street, Santa Monica; 451-5506.

Stampa Barbara Child's play? Hardly. This is sophisticated stuff. An incredible inventory of over 60,000 rubberized images and designs, along with neon inkpads, glitter glue, embossing powder, and everything else imaginable to help you stamp your art out. 6903 Melrose Avenue, LA; 931-7808.

Fantasies Come True A den of Disneyana and they're not mousing around. This store should be declared a museum. Owner Bob Molinari has managed to find (and keeps on finding) the cream of collectibles, including character figurines and cels. Be it $3 keychains or $3,000 Capodiamonte recreations of entire scenes from movies, there's anything and everything a former Mouseketeer could wish upon a star for. 8012 Melrose Avenue, LA; 655-2636.

Dudley Do-Right Emporium Major moose madness—stuffed Bullwinkles and antler baseball caps, for example—and a myriad of exclusive merchandise marketing the best (and rest) of Jay Ward's cartoon clan. Not to be missed: original scripts and cels (at great prices, too), Dudley wristwatches and cassette recordings of the "Rocky," "George of the Jungle," and "Super Chicken" theme songs. Basics no professional Baby Boomer should be without. 8200 Sunset Boulevard, Hollywood; 656-6550.

Have a Nice Day Sensational '60s stuff, from plastic living room sets and lava lamps to happy face patches and Peter Max blowup pillows. Drop by, turn on (an eight-track player), tune in. 7021 Melrose Avenue, LA; 936-8070.

The Rock Store Everything an antique store isn't, and everything an LA antique store should be—fun, funky, and nothin but rock 'n roll memorabilia. You'll find autographs, original stage clothing, 15,000 posters, and entire sections devoted to Elvis (with over 500 pieces, most of which—like the Elvis Christmas decorations and the Elvis salt and pepper shakers—were previously only available at Graceland), the Stones, the Monkees, and the Beatles. Money can't buy you love, but it will buy you bobbing-head dolls, Fab Four lunch boxes, and genuine Beatles' wigs. 6817 Melrose Avenue, LA; 930-2980.

Yesterday Once Again More nostalgia—a large and varied collection of antique phonographs, ranging from the simple and austere to the more colorful and grand. Plus a sizable selection of both flat-disc and cylindrical records, so you can make all kinds of beautiful music. By appointment only; (714) 963-2474.

House of Hermetic Are you a good witch or a bad witch? Even if you're not a witch at all, you can find everything you would want or need, like crystal balls and tarot cards, plus incense, candles, herbs, and oils. 5338 Hollywood Boulevard, Hollywood; 466-7553.

Selected Readings

Larry Edmunds Books about cinema and the theater (including rare and out-of-print editions) as well as stills and posters; said to have been Truffaut's favorite place in LA. 6658 Hollywood Boulevard, Hollywood; 463-3273.

Samuel French The play's the thing. Great theater books, too. 7623 Hollywood Boulevard, Hollywood; 876-0570.

Hennessy & Ingalls Books and magazines on art, architecture, photography, furniture, and design, plus prints and calendars (and a great facade by Morphosis). 1254 Santa Monica Mall, Santa Monica; 458-9074.

Artworks Original, artist-designed books, including flip books, pop-ups, hand-painted pages, die-cut covers, and lots of unique stuff. 170 S. La Brea Avenue, Hollywood; 934-2205.

Art Catalogs Just what the name says. Thousands and thousands of catalogs of contemporary art and photography exhibits (Impressionism to the present) from museums around the world. 625 N. Almont, Beverly Hills; 274-0160.

Scene of the Crime A mecca for mystery lovers with over 10,000 spy thrillers, detective stories, and whodunits in stock. 13636 Ventura Boulevard, Sherman Oaks; (818) 981-CLUE. **Sherlock's Home** offers an equally outstanding selection, plus some fun mystery-related goods. Check out the gargoyle-shaped bookends and the guide map to "Raymond Chandler's LA." 4137 E. Anaheim Street, Long Beach; 494-2964.

A Change of Hobbitt Speculative fiction: science fiction, fantasy, and horror. The sales help actually can. 1853 Lincoln Boulevard, Santa Monica; GREAT-SF (473-2873). Also worth your while: **Dangerous Visions,** 13603 Ventura Boulevard, Sherman Oaks; (818) 986-6963.

Children's Book and Music Center Talk about a baby boom. There are currently close to two dozen stores in the greater LA area specializing in books and things for kids. This one is the oldest; the more than 20,000 titles also makes it the biggest and the best. 2500 Santa Monica Boulevard, Santa Monica; 829-0215. Still the others, particularly the **San Marino Toy and Book Shoppe** (818-795-5301), shouldn't be ignored. For a detailed listing, contact **Southern California Children's Booksellers Association**, P.O. Box 2895, La Jolla, CA 92038.

Bodhi Tree Room after room of books on the new age, holistic health, spiritualism, mysticism, metaphysics, and enlightenment, as well as incense, meditation tapes, and prisms, all of it to help you raise your karmic consciousness. 8585 Melrose Avenue, W. Hollywood; 659-1733. **The Phoenix Bookstore** has a similar selection, but with some fiction and a choice stock of used books in the basement. 514 Santa Monica Boulevard, Santa Monica; 395-9516.

Sisterhood Bookstore Books by, for, and about women, with an emphasis on women's health, history, and psychology. There is also a good choice of nonsexist and nonracist children's books. 1351 Westwood Boulevard, Westwood; 477-7300.
Similar stores: **Bread and Roses,** 13812 Ventura Boulevard, Sherman Oaks; (818) 986-5376; and **Page One,** 966 N. Lake, Pasadena; (818) 798-8694.

A Different Light A vast choice of small-press fiction, nonfiction, and magazines both about and of interest to gays and lesbians. 4014 Santa Monica Boulevard, Silverlake; 668-0629.

La Cité des Livres French books and magazines, plus a good stock of Michelin maps and guides. 2306 Westwood Boulevard, Westwood; 475-0658.

Kinokuniya Bookstore Japanese fiction, history, philosophy, and travel books—and all of it in English. New Otani Hotel, 110 S. Los Angeles Street, Downtown; 687-4447.

Amok Bookstore An eclectic selection from out-of-the-mainstream small publishing houses, including how-to books on terrorism, torture, UFOs, secret societies, cults, plus lots of other weird stuff. 1067 North Hyperion Avenue, Silverlake; 665-0956.

Made to Order

15

A catalog of uniquely personal gifts

Next time you feel the temptation to give in and give them a blender, a necktie, or a bottle of perfume, *just say no.* Make their day and make their **Dreams Come True** (661-1300). For five years, John Alexander and his staff of erstwhile fairy godmothers have been working magic, granting wishes, and arranging for almost anything, from captaining a 747 to cooking one-on-one with Wolfgang Puck. And that's only the beginning. Those box seats at the Bowl? The chance to assistant coach the Rams? A walk-on on a favorite soap? It can be done. Choose from a clever list of prepackaged pamperings (starting at $75) or spill the beans and they'll arrange to have a secret fantasy fulfilled—as long as it's fun, legal, ethical, and doesn't require an act of God. No way even Uncle Leon would think of returning this one.

Your Wish Is Their Command ▎

Although they rank high on the sentimental scale, photographs hardly make original gifts. But **Don's Camera** (10662 Riverside Drive, Toluca Lake; 818-766-4216) can take even the most bland family photo and make it come alive. Simply supply him with a favorite print, slide or negative (or set up an appointment and he'll shoot exactly what you need) and two weeks (and $25 to $40) later, he'll give it back, only laminated on acrylic, die-cut, and mounted on a base. The result is an unusual, two-dimensional, stand-up portrait that stands out in any crowd.

Your Face Here ▎

Artist **Robert Ray** (664-5233) can take a favorite image and take it one step further, working from it to capture the person of your choice in sculpted 3-D form. For $200, Ray studies photos, gathers facts, and uses both to flesh out humorous clay caricatures—foot-tall, full-figure cartoon statues that are clever, cool, and just as fun as the California Raisins. . . .

Which is all well and good, but suppose it's more essential that you simply make a big impression? Then picture this: a treasured snapshot blown up to poster size, one where the color, clarity, and quality are as good as the original. The folks at **Jetgraphix Services** (1531 Pontius Avenue, West LA; 479-4994) can do exactly that and more, thanks to ink-jet printing capabilities and a hi-tech computer image system. But how isn't as important as what, and the possibilities here are endless: photos, slides, postcards, illustrations, personal documents, newspaper clippings, even covers of books, magazines, and albums; all reproduced in larger-than-life form and suitable for framing. Costs run from $59 to $139, with foam core mounting and shipping tubes available.

What the Hawaiian shirt is to Honolulu, the satin baseball jacket is to LA—slick, stylish, exclusive, and a symbol of Hollywood affiliation. But cast and crew aren't the only ones who can wear their credits on their sleeves. **LP Designs** (10513 Burbank Boulevard, N. Hollywood; 818-980-6042 or 213-877-6940) has custom-created promotional and commemorative clothing for all the industry biggies, and they'll only too happily do it to order for you. While renowned for their embroidery, they also screen, airbrush, and handpaint; and not just on satin jackets, but on every garment imaginable, from sweats and windbreakers to pillows, blankets, and even upholstery. Best of all, they don't demand that you order 100 as opposed to one, and prices start as low as $24 to $30. Hooray for Hollywood.

Your Table Is Waiting

If the trendy new furniture store has you frustrated because their definition of custom-made means showing you a catalog and letting you pick the color, style, or fabric, then tell them to sit on it and give **John Wilson** (714-492-6399) a call. Wilson isn't an interior designer, but he does design one-of-a-kind furnishings—mainly soft-sculptured, hand-painted sofas, love seats, and chairs—and has crafted them to look like everything from a Porche 911 to a king-size chili cheeseburger (where a side of fries and a glass of Coke double as arm and back rests). Imagine buying a typewriter couch for the office or commissioning a high-heel chaise lounge for the bedroom. Simply decide what you want and from models of the real thing, his studio will draw up plans showing you how they can transform a favorite object into a functional piece of art. Figure production time to take about a month from start to finish, and figure if you have to ask the price, you probably can't afford it.

You're History

Clever, cheap (How cheap? Try $6), looks like you went all out to come up with something special, and available at the last minute. Sound like the perfect birthday gift? Then celebrate their life with *Life,* and get them the issue that was published the week they were born. At the **Westwood Collector Exchange** (1087 Gayley Avenue, Westwood; 208-8416) you'll find a library of back issues of the famous weekly and not just a select few, but a comprehensive stock spanning 1936 to the present. And that's just for starters. Mixed in are files filled with quality-condition copies of *The Saturday Evening Post, Colliers, Time, Fortune,* and countless fashion magazines, each offering a unique way to say "Have a happy" or to take an anniversary couple on a nostalgia-filled trip down memory lane.

You'll need to allow five days shipping time, but similarly, **The Authentic Journal** (537-8101 or 800-343-7488, ext. 59), based in Rancho Dominguez, mail-orders whole copies of dozens of US newspapers: *The New York Times, The Los Angeles Times, The San Francisco Chronicle,* and *The Washington Post,* among them. Their collection dates back 100 years, so don't think this is a Xerox, photostat, or reproduction—what you'll get is the original thing. Available three ways: as is ($30), in a leatherette cover ($65), or bound ($90).

16

Culture for Sale

*One-of-a-kind artists' goods
from a slew of one-of-a-kind places*

Freehand The contemporary crafts shop that set the standards for comparison. From stunning blown glass with applied decorations, to beautiful painterly ceramics, to arty jewelry and exquisite hand-woven (raw silk) clothes, this place is two rooms of solid proof that good taste *can* be bought. 8413 W. Third Street, LA; 655-2607.

New Stone Age The least conservative of all the stores showcasing artist-designed goods. It constantly surprises, but expect to find an emphasis on alternative materials (baskets woven out of telephone wire, bottle-cap jewelry, black matte tin cans, and metal kitchen utensils that have been converted into lamps) as well as handsome glass plates and platters trimmed in platinum or gold, jazzy sequined picture frames, and a nifty supply of very silly salt-and-pepper shakers. While located next door to Freehand, the two stores are careful not to overlap in stock, allowing them to complement rather than compete. 8407 W. Third Street, LA; 658-5969.

Wilder Place I never saw an item here I didn't want. Copper and oxidized-metal bowls and vases, old TV sets that double as aquariums, hand-painted screens, concrete phones, marble fruits, bleached-out wooden platters, and mix 'n match pastel-colored pottery. Owner Jo Wilder should have her eye for buying insured with Lloyd's of London. This is the kind of stuff that *Metropolitan Home* is made of. 7975 Melrose Avenue, LA; 655-9072.

Tops Dazzle yourself into delirium. Every nook, cranny, wall, shelf, case, and countertop is piled high and lined full, showcasing a soup-to-nuts selection of unique (though not cheap) artist-crafted things. Among them: Jim Wagner's terrific hand-painted weathered furniture (they had it *before* Santa Fe was in), kids' chairs designed to look like animals (the skunk, by the way, doubles as a potty seat), and cabinets and tables made from planks from 19th-century farmhouses. Plus rugs, mirrors, picture frames, jewelry, toy art, and ceramics—from the superhip to the sublime. Did I mention the squirrel monkey bank that sticks its tongue out when you deposit money? The kitchen clock with a breakfast setting for the face and two bacon strips as hands? The flying fish portal . . . ? 23410 Civic Center Way, Malibu; 456-8677.

Craft and Folk Art Museum Gift Shop Collectibles tied in with current shows, plus stock that changes weekly, makes this one of the choicest shopping spots in town. The sculptural ceramics (vases, bowls, pots) are varied and outstanding. So are the artisan-designed dolls, the Mexican and African masks, the hand-dyed baskets, the mix of fine art and ethnic jewelry, and the huge library of books on craft and folk art. Fail to find a gift here and your charge cards should be cancelled. 5814 Wilshire Boulevard, LA; 937-9099.

MOCA Book Store Pop-culture books, hand-marbled stationery, and other keenly chosen mass-produced products share space with a well-thought-out selection of art and gift art, all of it wild, wonderful, and (get this) surprisingly affordable. The kids' toys (rolling city skylines and hi-tech interlocking free forms) are inspired. The textured concrete bowls, brightly painted stash boxes, and Parthenon-modeled bird houses are definitely hard to resist. And Katrin Wiese's amusing new-wave wood sculpture "Smith Family" character pieces are, in and of themselves, reason alone to stop by. Everything a museum store should be, and more. 250 S. Grand Avenue, Downtown; 621-2766, ext. 710; branch store at The Temporary Contemporary, 152 N. Central.

Taylor-Gratzer Entering this bi-level gallery/store, with its wacky bigger-than-life-size 3-D figures, whimsical multimedia plateaus, and humorous art that functions as furniture, is akin to stepping into the Sunday funny pages. New shows are set up monthly (so artists and works vary), but rarely is there a teapot or soup tureen in sight. Figure the focus to be on large-scale pieces that are offbeat, accessible, and fun. You'll be amused by Laurie Warner's cactus chairs . . . do a double take at Susan Seaberry's sofas painted to appear as if there are people sitting on them . . . come nose-to-toes with Mark Beam's six-foot cow balancing upside down on the world. And, like me, wish you could have them all. 8605 Sunset Boulevard, W. Hollywood; 659-6422.

Also worth checking out is **Wild Blue** (7220 Melrose Avenue, LA; 939-8434), a little shop that's big on humor. Prominently displayed are cartoon-colored ceramics (such as chili pepper–dotted dinner plates), lifelike porcelain renditions of simple, everyday artists' objects (pencils, paintbrushes, or drawing pens, for starters), and serving bowls that sport portraits of stressed-out party-goers (proclaiming sentiments like, "Hey man, the cocktail nuts are history," and "I'm gonna kill the fat dude who ate all the bean dip."). Good for a laugh and a good source for gifts that are clever without being cute.

Over the years, the Taos, NM–based **Sonrisa** has spawned a host of so-so imitators, but finally (thankfully), has an LA offshoot of its own. Known for their amazing array of Mexican folk art, folk crafts, antiques, and jewelry, the new store (8214 Melrose Avenue, LA; 651-1090) has that and more, including interesting furniture pieces from northern New Mexico and ceramic works by local Hispanic artists.

Tesoro (319 S. Robertson Boulevard, LA; 273-9890) is like a mini-department store of artful shopping, ideal when you need to buy a gift, but have no idea what you're looking for. Located in the hub of the decorator showrooms, here you're sure to discover something for any style of home. The floor-to-ceiling displays come brimming, abundant with flatware, textiles, pottery, and china, as well as cases of colorful jewelry, stylish picture frames, and architectural accent pieces.

An equal-parts gallery and store, **Del Mano** (11981 San Vicente Boulevard, Brentwood; 476-8508; and 33 E. Colorado Boulevard, Pasadena; 818-793-6648), has evolved into a principal showcase for contemporary American crafts, making for a terrific place to browse as well as buy. But buy is what you'll probably want to do as they feature a broad range of products in a broad range of prices, including a plethora of fine art/precious metal jewelry. Nothing seems to be right? Consider commissioning any one of the artists represented to do exactly what you want.

When Sending a Card Isn't the Very Best

17

Alternative ways to get your message across

Patrick Media Group (731-5111). *Cost:* $555/month. **On a Billboard**
Details: Over 7,000 billboards in the LA area alone.
Demand for westside spots is at a premium—if that's the
location you want, you'll probably have to settle for something in Hollywood or mid-Wilshire instead; will do the
artwork for you or can work from your designs, as long as
they are camera-ready and to scale.

Winston Network (383-7495). *Cost:* $110–$175/month, **On the Side of**
depending on size and where sign is posted on bus. **a Bus**
Details: Space available on all RTD buses as well as
Orange County, Torrance, San Bernardino, and Santa
Monica lines; will not guarantee a particular bus, only a
particular route; finished artwork (on vinyl) must be provided (contact Colby Poster Printing, 747-5108). Winston
also leases Jr. Billboards (6' x 12'), most commonly used
to advertise movies, for $155. Colby is capable of provid-
ing the eight-sheet needed for these as well (production
cost is $175).

Special Occasions Songs (396-5706). *Cost:* $500. **In a Song**
Details: You give them the details and the background
information, and they'll provide custom lyrics and music,
tailored to any event, day, or occasion. From romantic
ballads to novelty songs.

Video Greetings (818-885-7887). *Cost:* $10. *Details:* **In a Video**
Setup is similar to the old-fashioned "Take Your Own
Photo" booth; special cassettes run 10 minutes and play
on any VHS machine; prerecorded greetings for the
holidays are also available—you simply add a personal
message at the end.

Main on Foods (727-7100). *Cost:* $78/case. *Details:* **Inside a Fortune**
Prefers minimum orders of five cases (figure on 3,250 **Cookie**
cookies); you'll probably have to beg, but single, giant-
sized cookies can be custom-made on request. Their per-
ishable nature makes them impossible to ship, so better
your chances by offering to pick one up directly from
the factory.

With a Box of Candy

BBC Candy (675-6178). *Cost:* $5.95/pound. *Details:* This is English hard-rock candy—made in a long roll and then sliced, so the message runs through each piece, not just across the top; minimum order of 50 pounds is required, making it (as well as the fortune cookies) best suited for promotional purposes and party favors.

High in the Sky

Sky Advertising (592-3068 or 714-846-2118). *Cost:* $275–$450, depending on where you need it done. *Details:* Display (including banner, smoke, honking horns, and music) lasts 15 to 20 minutes; plane passes back and forth over designated location six times; beach areas provide best vantage point since pilot is able to fly lower.

Spelled Out

Sky Typers (598-8577). *Cost:* $650, assuming planes are already scheduled to be in air. *Details:* Five planes jointly type out messages running up to 20 characters in length. (Each letter stands as tall as the Empire State Building; visibility stretches for 20 miles.) Old-fashioned, one-plane skywriting is also available, but it's best suited for simple logos, symbols, or five-to-six-letter words.

In Lights

Pyro-Spectaculars (714-874-1644). *Cost:* $600 and up (and up), based on needs, location, and permit requirements. *Details:* Small-scale, specially constructed set pieces can be commissioned with graphic words, logos, characters, scenes, and even animation reproduced in fire; an impressive list of credits includes Disneyland, Disney World, and the '84 Olympics.

Say It With Food

18

*Whether you're saying "thank you"
or "thinking of you," food is the
consummate gift. There's no need
to worry about size or color;
only a fool would think, "Oh, we
already have one"; and if it's
good, who's going to care that you
sent the same thing last year?*

You'll definitely tickle their taste buds (and show off
your good taste) with stylish deliveries from **Angeli**
(287-1771)—handsome, hand-packed baskets that come
laden with a smorgasbord of Italian sweets and eats.
The selection varies, but starts with cheese, salami, and
bottles of olive oil and balsamic vinegar; then inevitably
mixes fresh pasta and freshly baked, chocolate-pistachio
or cinnamon-raisin *biscotti,* and with the restaurant's sig-
nature *panini* (little loaves of bread made from their
incomparable pizza dough) heading the list.

Basket Cases

Used to be that great buns could only be gotten in various
gyms and health clubs around town, but thanks to
Bodacious Buns (Century City Marketplace; 551-2867),
now anyone can have them. Whether your choice is cinnamon raisin, cinnamon chocolate chip, or cinnamon orange
pecan, baskets of these colossal confections are available
for delivery—ooey, gooey, and warm from the oven—anywhere in LA. They'll throw in fresh-ground coffee, assort-
ed teas, and cinnamon candies if you want, but be a real
friend and opt for extra buns instead.

Old family recipes and pure old-fashioned goodness are
the main ingredients of the gift baskets and decorative
tins from **Mrs. Beasley's** (19572 Ventura Boulevard,
Tarzana; 818-344-7845; also at Fred Segal Santa Monica;
394-6983). These local favorites come piled high with
minimuffins, bar cookies, brownies, chewies, tea cakes,
jams, and fruit butters, each better than the next, and any
one of them perfectly moist and wonderful. You can order
by phone or by mail, but the best way to order is in person, because free tasting and sampling is encouraged.

As the name implies, **Unforgettable** (477-4479) makes
memorable chocolate chip cookies. But so do Bonnie,
Lisa, Blue Chip, David, Famous Amos, and Mrs. Fields.
Which may explain why eight years ago, rather than open

yet another cookie store, they started baking theirs with wire stems attached and packaging them in groups of twelve in oblong floral boxes. Today, long-stemmed c-c-c's are not uncommon in LA. But while possibly old hat, they are certainly no less delicious; and since virtually unheard of elsewhere, highly recommended when needing something novel for someone out of town.

Gertie's (10113 Washington Boulevard, Culver City; 837-2253) also serves up edible bouquets, offering designer baby cheesecakes creatively packaged in a range of floral boxes. Baked from a recipe that has been in the family for three generations (and was once served at the Brown Derby by Gertie's mother Ray), these are clearly California cheesecakes—light, creamy, and available in a gluttony of incarnations, ranging from chocolate raisin and root beer float to margarita and mocha Grand Marnier (named, by the way, to honor the MGM Studios across the street).

Why settle for a liquor store–style gift basket, filled with wine and cheese, when for the same price ***Perfect Picnics*** (627-2981) will pack—and hand-deliver—a classic picnic basket with that and much, much more? Chilled fresh juices, still-hot bagels, homemade jams and jellies, and food enough for two are among the special touches that add to their originality and charm.

And strange as it may sound coming from the King of Carbohydrates, it is the combination fruit and vegetable basket from ***Stanford Gift Baskets*** (626-4438) that could be the most spectacular gift-to-eat in town (or out of town, since they will readily deliver anywhere). Put together by Northern Produce Company, whose clients include Spago, Trumps, the Ritz-Carlton, and Royal Viking Cruise Lines, these exquisite woven willow baskets overflow with everything that's healthy, exotic, trendy, and gourmet: champagne grapes, golden raspberries, fresh herbs, baby carrots, tiny eggplants, cavaillon melons, pleurotte mushrooms, and on and on, depending on the season. Harry and David should be ashamed.

House Callers

19

*Check into a hotel and the first
thing you're apt to do is order room
service. Never mind that a cup of
coffee costs five bucks; there's something
to be said about just picking up the
phone and having whatever you could
want brought directly to you. But
why have to camp out at a Four Seasons
to enjoy all this comfort? Good news,
couch potatoes: you don't. There's lots
more to at-home delivery services
than pepperoni pizza and
Fuller brushes. Witness. . . .*

The Auto Agent Getting a new car is a joy; buying it, however, can be hell. So let Ed Scher face the pushy salesmen for you. After an initial phone call to find out what you want (or to help you make up your mind), he'll hunt down the perfect model-match, set up a test drive, do the comparison shopping, take care of the extras (car phones, stereos, alarms, extended warranties), assure financing, and arrange delivery. Directly to your home or office. All you do is sign on the dotted line . . . and (oh, there is a God) save a lot of money in the process. 207-3607.

Cars R Us

Bundle of Convenience New Parent Law #183: The later into the night that the baby wakes up needing a change, the greater the chance that there won't be any diapers in the box. Well, beat the odds and sleep easy. Tobey Costen and Mark Seigel offer regularly scheduled home delivery (usually once every-other week) of more than 100 different baby-care products, from basic bottles to hard-to-find all-cotton wipes. What sounds like an indulgence straight out of *thirtysomething* carries a price tag that even Michael and Hope couldn't whine about: figure 15 percent over normal grocery-store costs, with a minimum of $35 requested. Special one-time orders, Orange County service, or UPS delivery for families who plan to travel can also be arranged, making it all the easier to Pamper the baby while you pamper yourself. 839-1114 or (818) 376-1114.

Baby Carry-age

And just as BOC will see that the kids are diapered and fed, a visit from **Mr. Baby Proofer** (818-763-3900) makes sure that they're safe and secure. No more crying over spilt formula. Danny McNeill will stop by, survey the house, point out what could be a potential danger and give you a free estimate detailing what he can do to correct it. Rates vary depending on your needs, but jobs commonly include latches for cabinets and drawers, gates for stairways, and plexiglas for open bannisters, as well as toilet locks and outlet covers.

Clothes to Home

The Bonnie Roseman Co. Face it. You may have been born to shop, but you could easily die fighting the crowds or waiting for someone semi-intelligent to help you. Enter Bonnie and Alan Roseman. A stash of leather suitcases in tow—crammed with everything that's new and different in women's clothing and accessories—they simply bring the store to you. Once inside, Alan starts to unpack, while Bonnie, doubling as saleswoman/model, strips down to a black body stocking, then dons and doffs what they've brought along to show you how it looks. And how it looks is outstanding: hand-sculpted earrings, cashmere capes, metal-mesh tops, jeweled tuxedo jackets, plus all sorts of leathers, suedes, and knits, from hot to haute to hip. So what if the typical sale averages 1,000 bucks? At least you can say there's not an average piece of clothing in the bunch. 208-6188.

In recent years, eyeglasses have given way to "eyewear," evolving as a major fashion statement. **Starry Eyes** (271-1999 or 818-981-4851) allows you to see and be seen with the best, offering an eclectic selection of over 500 fashionable frames to choose from. The $50 house call is applicable towards purchase; custom designs along with the more traditional optical services (hand-tintings, coatings, etc.) are available.

Couched Answers

LA Design Concepts You need a new couch. Yet shopping the furniture stores can be frustrating, not to mention a total waste (just try finding any of the great stuff you've seen in the magazines). So what's a person without a decorator or a resale number to do? Send Frank Keshishian the picture, that's what. His design firm will track down any item featured and handle all purchasing, expediting, and delivery, no minimum required. In just a matter of weeks (and for only 15 percent over wholesale), you and yours can be sitting pretty. 276-2109.

Specific Pacific A neighborhood butcher shop on wheels, operating door to freezer door, dishing out restaurant-quality meats and seafood (as well as pre-prepped appetizers and entrees, though some of these tend to be a little salty). Beef's the best bet, be it steaks, chops, or ribs. No double coupons, but no worrying about goods being sneakily packaged with the fatty side down, either. 328-8050.

Meat Tenders

The Flower Concierge Okay, okay. So no one brings you flowers anymore. Well, chin up, because Michael Gramatikos will. And not just a few stems or a stray spray either; we're talking the whole shop. From a mobile mart, he pedals petals directly to your door, stocking over 50 exotic varieties. A former flower wholesaler, this service blossomed from there, and though obviously a hit with the Beverly Hills hostesses, the low overhead makes it accessible to everyone. And that means for an average of $35 weekly, things really can look rosy. 935-6937.

Petal Pusher

Residential Services Good help isn't so hard to find, not when you call Wes Carlson. For 25 years, his company has served as a clearing house for competent, reliable, and fairly priced fix-it experts, from painters and plumbers to carpenters, contractors, and electricians. Simply tell him what you need done and he'll send over the best person to do it, then follow up to make sure it was done right. Any day of the week, 24 hours a day. 277-0770.

Have Staple Gun, Will Travel

The Clothes Hanger Kim Douglas will help you clean up your act, picking up your laundry and dry cleaning, hauling it away, and then bringing it back the next day, beautifully pressed, fluffed, and folded. Rates are comparable to what you'd pay taking it to the plant yourself. 818-766-8768. Likewise, **Mobile Cleaners** (655-0368) provides a multitude of dry cleaning services (not just clothes, but also bedding, draperies, and table linens) along with at-home fittings, alterations and tailoring, and all of it at competitive prices.

Pressed for Time?

To make sure you continue to look your best, **Pat Rico** (818-768-1358) can get the cardiovascular system going with a novel aerobic workout, coming to your home or office and teaching you how to tap dance. He's been instructing top Hollywood hoofers for over 30 years, and can have you ready for an MGM contract in no time.

Hire Tapping

People Who Do the Things You Hate to Do

Forget about skipping lunch so you can be first in line when the motor vehicles office reopens at one. For $10 to $15, **Tony's DMV Service** (818-447-2450) will handle your car registration problems for you. Just mail them the paperwork and they take care of the rest, whether it's emergency one-day re-registration or a simple transfer of title.

Time was when you didn't want to cook or didn't care to go out, there was little chance of eating well. But today, a slew of supermarkets as well as tonier take-out shops offer a glut of gourmet goods. At **A La Carte** (1915 S. Coast Highway, Laguna Beach; 714-497-4927), you could buy a pint of this and a half-pound of that, but it's the complete dinners (16 delicious choices cooked fresh daily, then prepackaged in containers suitable for freezing) that are the chief attraction. Along with the display case chock-full of a dozen different hors d'oeuvres, any one of them great, and all of them perfect for making entertaining unexpected company an unexpected ease. . . . And should the thought of even turning on the oven turn you off, take comfort in the knowledge that more and more restaurants now provide delivery service, though often within limited areas. For a detailed listing of who goes out and how far they go, pick up a copy of *LA Delivers,* available on newsstands or by subscription. Call 876-4545 for information.

Don't be kept in the dark. Give the word and **Legwork** (665-2449 or 876-1794), a veritable two-woman research library, will go to work for you, digging up scientific, historical, technical, and background information on just about anything. Geared towards helping the professional writer, they'll do it all: fill in the gaps, fact-check, synopsize existing materials, even go undercover—and do it fast, well, and with total confidentiality. What they *don't* do is answer simple questions on a single, one-time basis. But should you need to know the capital of Uganda, whose face is on the $100 bill, or when National Egg Salad Day is, you should know that the reference desks at many local libraries have most of the answers and will supply them over the phone. Among the best: **The Santa Monica Library Quick Reference Service** (451-8859).

And who said that you had to be big time, big business to have your own personal assistant? With **Executive Runaround** (734-4017, or 818-501-6466), anyone can delegate. For $15 an hour, they'll do everything you don't have the time to waste time doing, like take your car to be fixed, wait for the phone company, or meet your mother-in-law at the airport.

Lastly, if you've ever sworn that you would exercise religiously if only you had a personal trainer (secretly confident that you'd never have to follow through because at $75 to $100 an hour who could afford one?), well, sorry, the ruse is up. State-of-the-art private workout rooms at **Total Fitness** (856 S. Robertson Boulevard, Suite 200, Beverly Hills; 659-3341) are set up with three of every-thing, not only enabling one trainer to effectively handle three clients at the same time, but keeping your cost at just $25 for a 90-minute session. Meaning plenty of gain without the financial pain.

E

Parties, Hobnobbing, Social Climbing, and More

20 Ten Unusual Places to Throw a Party

1. On a Train

If you're worried about your guests just standing around and you really want to keep your party moving, **Classic Rail Travel** (714-633-0178) and **Golden Spike Rail Tours** (714-680-5090) can rent you a private railcar that will hook up with Amtrak and take you and your group for a one-day round-trip to San Diego, or on a weekend journey to San Francisco and back. Travel first class in a domed observation car from the 1950s or in a 1920s-style "Wild, Wild West" car complete with Victorian furnishings, observation platform, and Dixieland jazz band. Car rentals will run around $3,000 for 35 people and they'll throw aboard a chef and a porter as well.

2. Out at Sea

Shipboard weddings have long been a romantic favorite, and a party aboard a privately owned yacht is equally spectacular. **Blue Water Charter Concepts** (823-2676 or 301-8089) has dozens of ships available exclusively to them, including the 106-foot *Christabel*, which with three different decks, can accommodate a large buffet, dance floor, and 135 guests. Smaller yachts, like the *Mauretania*, can hold up to 50 people. For a 4-to-12-hour period, prices range from $850 to $4000, plus crew. And you'll even get to chart your own course.

3. At a Bowling Alley

With the current vogue for anything '50s, what better place for a family reunion, a Baby Boomer's 40th, or a "Big Chill" party? **Cafe Beignet** (234 Pico Boulevard, Santa Monica; 396-6976) is a vintage bowling alley/coffee shop, but a coffee shop with a nouvelle twist. Owner/chef Judy Binder apprenticed under Wolfgang Puck and her Americana fare is five-star down-home, echoing southern, creole, and truck-stop traditions. For groups of 50 or more, the chrome and formica eatery will close its doors to the public and arrange for you to use the adjacent bar and bowling alley.

4. At a Cooking School

If you're of the school that the essential ingredient to any great party is the food (and experience has proven that throwing one together always means too much work), then this one could have your name on it. No fussing over artistically cutting up the crudite, timing the souffle, or tracking down some weird ingredient here. All you have to do is show up. The **Epicurean Cooking School** (8759 Melrose Avenue, LA; 659-5990) will supply the room, the equipment, the groceries, and a well-known local chef (who's there depends on the type of party). Then you sit back and relax while he or she teaches and your guests do all the work.

5. On a Rooftop

Walk through the gates of the **Oviatt Building** (617 S. Olive, LA; 622-6096), bypass the city's most beautiful restaurant (but a peek inside should give you a hint of what's in store), then step into the carved-oak elevator and ascend to the 12th floor. You'll have to take the stairs to reach the 13th floor, but it only serves to make the entrance to your party more dramatic. Awaiting you is the 2500-square-foot deco penthouse and it (along with its period antiques, marble fireplaces, mahogany walls, Lalique glass, and sunken tubs) is yours for the evening. The apartment is perfect for cocktails and hors d'oeuvres, but the highlight is the 1500-square-foot rooftop terrace accessible only out your back door. Dine and dance under the stars and when the last of your guests has gone, you might be able to talk the management into letting you spend the night.

6. On a Carousel

Fairy tales sometimes do come true. Newly restored and completely refurbished, the **Santa Monica Pier Carousel** (Ocean and Colorado Avenues, Santa Monica; 394-7554), one of only a dozen hand-carved carousels in the country, can be yours any night after sundown. In addition to the magnificent merry-go-round (a full-time operator will be on hand, so everybody gets to ride), the building offers a festive 1920s setting, a sweeping view of the coastline, and room enough for as few as 50 or as many as 200 guests. A city permit is needed, as well as a certificate of insurance and possibly a fire marshall, but the whole shebang (which will easily run under $650) is well worth the extra hassle.

7. In an Ice Cream Factory

Rows of stainless steel shelving units are lined with chocolates, truffles, cookies, and other treats. A conveyor belt groans from the weight of too much ice cream. Pastry tubes oozing freshly made whipped cream are strewn about. And in the corner, a 20-gallon vat of semisweet hot fudge stirs continuously (finger tasting is encouraged). Sound like you've died and found Nirvana? Well, not quite. Nirvana in this case is the factory for

Robin Rose Ice Cream & Chocolates (215 Rose Avenue, Venice; 399-1774), but birthday parties don't get any better than this. The space does need to be decorated (some balloons plus a few shots of Lucy and Ethel in the chocolate factory should do the trick) but there is ample room for either tables and chairs or a disc jockey and dance floor.

8. In an LA Landmark

Who said an office party had to mean a nondescript conference room and a potluck dinner of spinach dip and tuna casseroles? Even if you don't work there, you can rent out the skylit open court and second floor mezzanine (perfect for dancing or just spying on your boss) of LA's unique **Bradbury Building** (304 S. Broadway, LA; 489-1893). We're talking brass fixtures, winding open stairs, oak walls, marble floors, and intricate wrought-iron railings, bannisters, and elevator cages. You almost expect to see Sam Spade leaving by the back door, ditching the landlord and hoping to buy a little time in order to cover the rent. . . . And if space is what you need, then the **Wiltern Theater** (3790 Wilshire Boulevard, LA; 388-1400), in all its art deco splendor, can accommodate 600 people on three levels. Guests will delight in sweeping down the lavish stairway (surely one of the grandest in all of LA) to a formal sit-down dinner in the foyer beneath the rotunda.

9. In a Museum

If you're bound and determined to see your party go down in history, then a good place to start is at the **Natural History Museum** (900 Exposition Boulevard, LA; 744-3337) where the dinosaurs and dioramas will play cohost to your guests. There's no minimum number of people required to book, but anything fewer than 150 would look lost in such a large area. . . . On a smaller scale, **The Museum of Neon Art** (704 Traction, Downtown; 617-1580), a gray cinder-block garage space filled with whimsical displays, will brighten up any party, but its availability is contingent on the artwork on display.

10. In Someone Else's Home

You'd love to give a party at home but home is a one-bedroom, prefabricated, stucco apartment. Call **Maralou Gray** (276-9262) and she'll arrange to give you someone else's home for the evening—from a Pasadena Victorian to a cliffside medieval castle to Liberace's estate. Pictured in Gray's portfolio are dozens of mansions in the LA area, most of which are lived in and completely furnished. Rents average around $3,000, but party activities are not restricted to the courtyards or lawns; you'll have full use of the house, the kitchen, the ballroom, the music room, the library, the greenhouse, the parlor...

21

Best Bets for Parties

Best Bet for Flowers

Bloomsbury Flower Market Well-known for having the lowest prices for the most unusual and exotic selection west of the Flower Mart, Bloomsbury has closed their retail doors, moved a few miles east, and now offers complete arranging and delivery services. Centerpieces, sprays, groupings, corsages—all first-rate and at 20 percent below anywhere else. 855-1001.

Best Bet for Something Other than Flowers

Balloonart by Treb Don't laugh. Not only can he delight your guests with a balloon launch, but this former Disneyland balloon boy is the first and foremost artist of his kind. Balloon sculptures (including letters that spell out guest of honors' names or numbers that reveal their ages) as well as columns, spirals, arches . . . even a balloon gazebo. It's all clever, colorful—and anything but "just for kids." 836-3121.

Roschu Ever wonder where caterers and party planners get all those wonderful props they use? Well, LA is an industry town and many of the prop houses available to the movie business are also open to the public. Liven up a birthday party with oversized toys and a giant rocking chair (shades of Edith Ann), turn your living room into a Greek temple (they offer lightweight columns and godlike statues on wheels), or humor the crowd with the likes of cartoon buzzards perched atop an eight-foot styrofoam cactus. And that's only the beginning. 6514 Santa Monica Boulevard, LA; 469-2749.

Best Bets for Helping Hands

Host Helpers You've done all the cooking yourself, but for once, you'd like to sit back and enjoy your own party. Host Helpers can send over anywhere from one to 100 college students, who for very reasonable rates will moonlight as waiters, bartenders, and clean-up crew. 478-7799.

Rent a Trash Bin Cleaning up doesn't bother you; having at least two dozen Hefty bags of trash—and knowing that the garbage man isn't due until Thursday—does. Still, no need to panic. This company will bring a dumpster to your home, leave it there overnight, and when it's full and ready the next morning, they'll come back to haul all your troubles away. 723-7000.

Jukeboxes for Rent Not only will it look great and is it cheap (under $200 for a vintage '50s Seeburg, slightly more for the classic Wurlitzer), but it will guarantee you the best selection of tunes (owner Don Muller stocks the 20 top hits from every year from the '40s to the present), and you won't have to put up with the obnoxious patter of a would-be Wolfman Jack. (818) 366-9400.

But if your search is for something quieter, then why not a harpist, a flutist, or a string quartet? The music departments at **Cal State Northridge, Cal Arts,** and any number of other local universities offer lists of top students who are available to play at private parties. Incredible talent for not a lot of money.

22

There's No Place Like Home

*Ways to entertain that
will take you no further than
your own backyard*

Just Desserts

Eighty-six the appetizers, skip the salad, bypass the main course, and get straight to the good stuff. (Hey, nothing succeeds like excess.) A dessert-only buffet is opulent, extravagant, lavish, and incredibly cheap to do well. But before you pull out all the cookbooks or go in search of the perfect treats, give **The Venice Patisserie** (13375 Beach Avenue, Venice; 306-4280) a call. Pastry chef-wonder Amy Pressman (formerly of Spago and Pasadena's Parkway Grill) wholesales some of the best desserts in town to countless well-known restaurants; better yet, she'll also sell to you. Included in her repertoire are over 60 incredible creations—stuff you won't find in just any corner bakery, stuff that tastes as outstanding as it looks, stuff with names like Zebra Cake and Almond Roca—and all of it stuff you can buy at cost. Line a table with a dozen or so of these delights and you're guaranteed a party that, come the next morning, will still be on everybody's lips.

**Weekend
Eggstravaganza**

Liven up a Sunday brunch and ease your own workload with the help of **The Omelette King** (818-780-9943). John Vernon will don a tuxedo and bring his class act to your kitchen, dining room, or poolside patio, handling two pans at once and serving up a menu of gourmet choices, from chicken livers with fresh rosemary to artichokes in tarragon or caviar with sour cream. Build your own buffet around him or, with enough advance notice, he comes equipped with bagels, croissants, juice, coffee, and champagne. A great idea for a late night (after the theater, after the game) supper party as well.

**East Coast
Traditional**

You don't have to live in New England, let alone anywhere near the beach, to enjoy a genuine Cape Cod clambake. All you need is a phone. **Seafood Emporium** (19762 Ventura Boulevard, Woodland Hills; 818-347-4350) stocks all the necessities—live lobsters (no chick lobsters, only the best), clams (ask for softshell steamers), ears of corn, baby new potatoes, and seaweed—and will pack them in aluminum stove-proof pans (cole slaw and clam chowder included on the side) to go. No hole to shovel, no bonfire to build; just turn up the heat (either oven or BBQ grill) and 30 minutes later, dig in.

Okay, okay . . . so a barbecue in LA is about as common as actors waiting tables. But not to worry. If you can't wow them with the concept, wow them with the food. For over 50 years, **Noonan's** (6601 S. Western Avenue) has been supplying top-rate baby back pork ribs, beef ribs, chickens, hams, and turkeys (all of them marinated in honey and spices, then hickory-smoked in custom-made brick ovens) to local restaurants, hotels, butcher shops, and markets—who, in turn, just heat and serve, and then pass them off as their own. What's great is that you, too, can do the same. The Pit (752-0032), a small retail outlet located alongside Noonan's, offers all of their products to the public—by the pound and at the same price (40 percent off) that it sells them to the trade. Fire up the grill, place everything on just as the guests arrive, and for once you'll be able to have a party without having to spend all your time basting, turning, and slaving over the hot coals.

Roll up the shirt sleeves, grease back your hair and treat the neighborhood, the family, or 200 of your closest friends to a '50s evening of burgers, fries, and rock 'n roll. Happy Days are here again, thanks to the folks at **In and Out** (818-338-5587), who offer a "rolling hamburger stand" that comes directly to your home. The prices are the same as what you would be charged at any of their locations, but since the truck's cooking facilities are minimal, your menu will be limited to burgers, chips, and soda. But don't let that disturb you. Let **Let's Have a Cart Party** (839-6749) supply you with one or two street-vendor-style pushcarts to dish out whatever else you want, be it fries and shakes or chili dogs and cherry Cokes. And as for music, the vintage Seeburg is only a phone call away (see **Jukeboxes for Rent**, "Best Bets for Parties"). But best of all, you can do all this, for as little as $6 a person.

23 — Private Rooms for Private Parties

If company celebrations, charity lunches, or bridal and baby showers conjure up images of rubber chickens in boring banquet rooms, think again. Here are some tasty—and tasteful—alternatives:

Chez Helene Hearty French country cooking in an overgrown country kitchen environment that looks more like the South of France than South Beverly Drive. Their charming side room is all exposed brick, polished wood, and fresh flowers and will handle up to 40 people, although half that number can easily fill the same space. The back-to-basics menu just oozes country comfort—from the escargot and the house pate to the leg of lamb or the world's best cream of tomato soup (and I don't even *like* tomato soup). 267 S. Beverly Drive, Beverly Hills; 276-1558.

Marix Tex Mex Playa Housed in a former sushi restaurant (the outside still reflects it), this funky '80s version of a Mexican cantina is hip, hot, happening, and loaded with sizzle (and not just from the platters of very good fajitas that go whizzing by). The upstairs room is perfect for a party of 15 to 35, and current renovation plans indicate that they will soon be able to handle more. Best of all, the portions are huge, the prices cheap, and the "kick-ass" margaritas pleasantly addictive.118 Entrada Drive, Santa Monica; 459-8596.

Women's Assistance League Tea Room Two years ago you would have choked on your blackened redfish before you would have been caught throwing a party here, but today, with its kitsch-covered walls and comfort food, the Assistance League Tea Room is the epitome of retro-chic. Although the blue-plate specials still attract a large clientele of blue-haired ladies (c'mon, that's half the fun), the finger sandwiches and chocolate fudge cake have passed the taste test of the Hollywood hip. Private rooms have folding walls, so are capable of handling anywhere from 10 to 300; special banquet menus are available. 1370 N. St. Andrews Place, Hollywood; 469-1973.

Rebecca's There's something paradoxical about entering a place so devoted to "see and be seen" and then being quickly ushered to a private room upstairs. But this is no ordinary restaurant (not with its Frank Gehry–designed interior of backlit oynx panels, floating crocodiles, and a glass octopus chandelier) and this is no ordinary private room. Though small (it will seat a maximum of 20 people), it seems to float out over the bar, giving you the best seat in the house and a bird's eye view of all the action on the floor. The food is also a feast for the eyes; you may order from the regular menu or work with the chef to design a meal of your own. Either way, you'll find it hard not to fill up on the chips; they're outstanding. 2025 Pacific Avenue, Venice; 306-6266.

Camelions Charm their socks off at this cozy bastion of quality California cooking. Once a private home, the design has basically been left intact, so it offers choice possibilities for special parties. Foremost are the several small rooms that flow off the central courtyard; with their whitewashed walls, adobe fireplaces, and quiet comfort, each has it own unique feel. But definitely worth checking out is the last room in the back: It opens up onto a private patio and is the perfect spot for taking advantage of the cool Santa Monica air. After all, when you've got it, you should flaunt it. 246 26th Street, Santa Monica; 395-0746.

Prego Lots of noise, lots of fun, lots of good food. A genuine trattoria, California-style (but not a kiwi pizza in sight). The room for rent upstairs is slightly more elegant, yet no less inviting—a blend of hardwood floors, long oak tables and contemporary art. At the Prego in Orange County, the menu is much the same, but the building is more grand—reminiscent of a Tuscan villa, and open and airy despite the office complex surroundings. Several rooms work perfectly for a party, particularly the glass-enclosed garden as well as the pastry kitchen (a personal favorite), where the marble worktable and industrial-sized ovens (when they're not in use) make for a novel setting. 362 N. Camden Drive, Beverly Hills; 277-7346; 18420 Von Karman Avenue, Irvine; (714) 553-1333.

Trumps The ultimate LA look (white beams, white walls, concrete tables) sets off the ultimate LA food (tamale du jour, potato pancakes with goat cheese and sauteed apples, a brie-and-grape quesadilla). No doubt Trumps is stylish—but it also goes down easy. And no time is this more evident than tea time. From the first bite of scone to the last sip of sherry, it's surprisingly traditional—and a cleverly cost-effective way to entertain or celebrate at one of the A-list spots in town. Three varying-sized private rooms are available. 8764 Melrose Avenue, W. Hollywood; 855-1480.

Minor Affairs

24

*Certain that there must be a better
way to celebrate your kid's
birthday than being trapped with
a dozen seven-year-olds in the
electronic frenzy of Chuck E. Cheese?*

Well, for starters you could turn your backyard into a petting zoo. **Rent-a-Pony** (818-341-2770) will truck over the full menagerie—pony, llama, sheep, goats, pigs, and ducks—each more at home than the family dog.

If your kids are ripe for adventure, **Imagine Chasing Rainbows** (556-5706) will create a treasure hunt within the confines of your own yard, with clues, prizes, and a pirate chest full of goodies, all designed to order.

If the fastest way to your kids' hearts is through their stomachs, then consider a sundae bar from **Dandy Don's** (818-992-4646)—gourmet ice cream, five wet toppings, 18 dry toppings, handmade cones, chocolate-covered bananas, and fresh fruit sorbets, all laid out on a make-your-own buffet.

Or you could reserve the workroom at **The Candy Factory** (12510 Magnolia Boulevard, N. Hollywood; 818-766-8220) where, straight out of Willy Wonka, your kids and their guests will be treated to a day of molding and shaping chocolates, as well as dipping strawberries, pretzels, and potato chips (the latter alone well worth the price of the party).

And if just getting the kids out of the house (and out of your hair) is your idea of heaven, then Phys. Ed. teacher Joy Richardson can organize one of her **Sports Parties** (634-4706 or 818-769-2473). With minimal clutter and maximum creativity, she will set up a mini-Olympics behind your house or at a neighborhood park, overseeing relay races, a water balloon toss, and an obstacle course, topped off by an awards ceremony and the blowing out of the candles on the cake.

25

Wanted: A Great Spot to Tie the Knot

Weddings are back, weddings are in, and weddings are everywhere. And in a city like LA where the sun shines most of the time, the most-wanted weddings are outdoors.

A Bride's Guide . . .

A good place to start looking would be at **Greystone Park** (905 Loma Vista Drive, Beverly Hills; 550-4654), former estate of oil tycoon E.L. Doheny, and 16 acres of beautifully manicured grounds. The 55-room stone Tudor mansion is closed to the public, but makes for impressive set decoration, along with the railed terraces, grassy slopes, and formal fountains and gardens.

Likewise, you could say "I do" in the shadow of a 1924 Renaissance-style masterpiece—**Muckenthaler Center** (1201 W. Malvern Avenue, Fullerton; 714-738-6340). You have two equally good choices here: the Italian gardens and palm court that overlook the valley, or a beautiful patio and gazebo. Ceremonies only, though; no receptions are allowed.

The schedule of availability is sporadic, but the huge sycamore tree and the handsome Moorish-tiled pools and patios surrounding the **Adamson House** at Malibu State Lagoon (23200 Pacific Coast Highway, Malibu; 456-9497) make for an ideal location, and the incredibly low prices (fees range from $125 to $250) might make it worth your while to be flexible with the date.

Seemingly out of place in the middle of a suburban housing tract, **Orcutt Ranch** (23600 Roscoe Boulevard, Canoga Park; 818-785-5798) is like a miniversion of the LA Arboretum, and the adobe ranch-house courtyard, the rose garden, and the grove alongside the stream are among the areas that can be roped off for a wedding. The only drawback could be that during your ceremony the park will still be open to the public, but each space is somewhat self-enclosed and a park ranger will be around to keep the curious away.

And if you can limit your guest list to 100 (and end the evening by 10:00 P.M.) then the **Wattles Mansion** (1824 N. Curson Avenue, Hollywood; 874-4005), an early 1900s mission-revival house with sloping front lawn and European terraced gardens, gives you the chance to take the plunge, Old Hollywood–style. The first floor of the mansion—recently renovated and restored—is included, and perfect for cocktails and a sit-down dinner; the back-yard patio and lawn are made to order for cutting the cake and dancing cheek-to-cheek.

Although a hotel might seem a ho-hum place to hold a wedding, several hold surprises. The sterile exterior of **The New Otani** (120 S. Los Angeles Street; 629-1200) doesn't hint at its exquisite rooftop Japanese garden—a tranquil setting, complete with pond, bridge, and water-fall, made more dramatic by the backdrop of office towers and distant highrise buildings.

Across town, the **Hotel Bel-Air** (701 Stone Canyon Road; 472-1211), though just minutes north of Sunset, is the embodiment of a storybook setting. (Trust me. Snow White didn't have it this good.) You'll pay a pretty price for such perfection, but with the stone patios, flowering gardens, and a wooden bridge over a babbling brook (filled with swans, no less), the only thing possibly miss-ing is the horse-drawn pumpkin carriage (though that, too, can surely be arranged).

If finding the perfect spot also means finding a nearby place to house your guests, then kill two birds with one buck (and save everyone a lot of money) by taking over the entire **Eastlake Inn** (1442 Kellam Avenue; 250-1620), a stylish eight-room Victorian turned B&B. The two of you can exchange vows in the neoclassical gazebo, host dinner in the dining room and parlor, and after you are wed and gone, your guests can stay over in the various antique-filled rooms and suites upstairs.

Similar types of operations can make similar arrange-ments. Definitely worth checking out is Catalina Island's stunning **Inn on Mt. Ada** (510-2030), though it should be you—and not one of your guests—who gets to spend the night in the Grand Suite, and **The Anaheim Coun-try Inn** (856 S. Walnut Street, Anaheim; 714-778-0150), an inviting 1910 Queen Anne mansion with nine rooms, a circular front porch, and an acre of beautiful gardens.

The right restaurant can make a wedding basically hassle-free; at least you don't have to fool with caterers, and since you'll be billed on a cost per person basis, there's usually no extra charge for the space. Only trouble is that what's on the table often takes second place to the type of table it's on. But not always. **The Saddle Peak Lodge** (419 Cold Canyon Road, Calabasas; 818-340-6029)—a rustic, overstuffed country retreat, with roaring fire-places, timbered walls, and handmade wooden furnishings—offers food that rivals the decor. The menu could best be described as California country, and although the kitchen places a heavy emphasis on game (such as venison, pheasant, and brook trout), a wide range of offerings, from steak stuffed with oysters to vodka-cured salmon, is available. Add to this a trilevel outdoor patio that rambles on, surveying the Malibu Canyon from every point.

And while it might seem an odd choice (hell, you have to pass a firing range to get there), the immediate area around the **Police Academy Club** (1880 N. Academy Drive; 222-9136) includes a small rock waterfall and rows of flowers in brick planters; and together with the adjacent banquet rooms, promises what could be the best wedding deal in town—a full buffet or sit-down dinner for $16.50 to $17.50 per person. The food is basic, but plentiful and good, and while it's not the Ritz, it's an environment worth considering.

Index